The Gospel
From A Four-Sided View

Written and illustrated by Jeff Todd

Introduction
By Lewis – The Common Tater

Reading the Bible freaks a lot of people out. Many feel that it's too complicated and should only be read by preachers or teachers and then translated so that they can understand it. Nope! That's the wrong way to look at it.

The fact is God's Word is for everybody. Anyone is able to make sense of it because God makes it possible through His Holy Spirit living within us. He will reveal spiritual things that apply to our life. For many of us, its just a matter of taking the time to open it up and read it.

If you knew that everything you needed to know about how to live life successfully was in there, wouldn't you want to read it for yourself? We also live in an age where people are listening to false doctrine and don't even know it. We don't take the time to compare what we are being told by preachers with what God's Word actually says. Many folks are being led astray. It's important to know the Truth! Try and think of the Bible as God's Words spoken directly to you on a personal level.

Since you have a copy of this book in your hand, you're probably wondering what it's all about. What's A BackPew Review? Right? If I had to give a quick answer, it's basically a simple man's perspective of what he receives from reading the Bible.

You see, I am an average ordinary person, just like you, that wants to live the Christian life the best way I can and hear what God is saying to me through His Word. I am basically writing

3

down my thoughts from what I learn from the Bible and through life in general. I have no worldly qualifications, certifications or doctrinations that makes me the man for the job. I am simple person – a nobody in the eyes of the world. However, I am saved and that makes me a child of God. And that's cool!

I also take the Great Commission seriously. Jesus told the disciples long ago to share the Gospel and take it to the four corners of the world. I feel that assignment was meant for us as well. Each one of us has a responsibility to let others know about Salvation – what it is and how to get it - and to tell someone what Jesus did for them on the cross.

For many of us, the questions are how do we do it and when can I get started? Right?

For me, I have to use what the Lord has given me. This includes the relationship I have with Jesus, His Word, and the gifts, talents, and characteristics that He molded into me from the day I was born. This also includes my ability to draw and write. Your gifts may be different, but are very important to God and should be used right away. And since Jesus is returning soon, the time you should begin sharing the Gospel is now.

I don't want you to get the wrong impression. The purpose of this book is not to be a substitute for reading the Bible. I feel everyone should read it. I don't want you to think I am poking fun at God's Word or trying to offend any religion. That's not my purpose. My hope and intentions for writing this book is that it will inspire you, as the reader, and will offer humorous illustrations to use in your walk with Christ. I want to put Christianity out there in a simple and easy-to-understand way so that everyone can get it. We can learn together how to live our life to its fullest with happiness and joy that God intended for us to live.

Hopefully, by reading this book, you'll see that being a Christian doesn't have to be boring and dull. I believe it should be energetic and alive like wired-up kids on a sugar high. We are to be a light in the world that we live in and shine out to others. When a person sees the way we are, it should make them want to be that way, too. Our lifestyle should point them to Jesus. Everything we say and do should reflect the One that saved us.

I have never considered myself to be like everyone else. The way I look at life may be different than the way others see it. Even as a young child, Christian people to me were always so serious and stiff-necked. It was almost like they were afraid to smile. I agree, it was wrong of me to segregate Christians like this, but those were the Christians I knew. As I grew older, I realized that some Christians were actually normal people and reflected Jesus in the way they acted.

I know from personal experience that being a Christian isn't hard. It's not a series of rituals or following a magic formula. It's actually so simple that anyone can be one. However, walking the Christian walk can be difficult and requires understanding of God's Word and applying it to our life. That's my purpose and focus of writing this book! I want to write something that would minister to people (no matter who they were) and possibly help them understand what it means to be a Christian and share with them the Gospel that leads them to eternal life.

It's got to be simple and easy to understand. I don't use BIG words when I speak, so I will not write BIG words when I am using this to reach people and lead them to Jesus. I can't! It's not how God made me! If you're reading this today, this book is for you from a simple-minded person like me. Being a Christian is awesome and it's not as weird as you may have heard. We're not crazy people! But, I am on a mission to show people how they can be saved.

One of the most important decisions we'll ever make is turning from our sinful nature and asking God for forgiveness. If you have never asked Jesus to come into your life, I hope and pray that you make that choice today.

Excuse me for a moment. I want to pray for you and for God's blessings on this book.

Dear Lord, I pray right now that You use these words from this book to reach people out there. Only You know who this is intended for and who will be reading this. I ask that you use it for Your glory and that this book will lead them to You. I give You all the praise and honor, Lord. Thank You for all that You do for me, Jesus. Amen.

This book is my personal commentary of the Gospel. These are scriptures that tell us everything about Jesus Christ – who He is, His teachings, His miracles and His parables. I am sure there are several books floating out there and sermons preached around the world, but this is what I received from doing my own personal study. It's a simple read.

If you find words that aren't spelled right, I'm sorry. If there are words left out, I apologize. This is about as good as it's going to get. I hope it is a blessing to you anyway and that you receive something from it.

So, here it is folks!

The Gospel
From A Four-Sided View

The Box

The first four books of the New Testament are considered the Gospels:

Gospel of Matthew
Gospel of Mark
Gospel of Luke
Gospel of John

You ever heard of them? They are called Gospels because they are written accounts of the life of Jesus Christ. There's four of them because they were written by four different fellas. They tell of His birth, His ministry, His death and His resurrection. It includes His teachings, parables, and several of His miracles, too. These books of the Bible are extremely important because they are like historical documents for folks to learn more about Jesus. It's not like we can all run down to our local courthouse and have them pull out His personal folder from their vault. They would have to point us in the direction of the Bible.

When I think of these four Gospels, I can't help but think of a box with Jesus being inside. Sounds kinda funny, I know. Outside this box, there are four fellas peeking in at Him from each of the four sides. Using their feathery pens and scrolly things, they write down their own personal thoughts, inspired by God of course, and they put it out there for others to read.

I imagine these guys had other things to do, like work or play camel golf, but they may have felt a 'calling' to do it. Ya know, one of those 'I can't sleep until I get this done' kinda thing. God used them for this purpose and preserved their writings to be available today. We're talking almost 2000 years later! Ain't that amazing?

Who were these writers of the Gospels? The Bible doesn't go into great detail into who they were. I couldn't find any birth records or job resumes, but I did get a little bit of tidbits about them. Here's what I found:

Matthew

Matthew was one of the original 12 apostles mentioned in the Bible. I'm sure he saw a lot of cool stuff that Jesus did. He witnessed the miracles, heard His teachings and even had dinner with Him a time or two. He had some firsthand experience. That's pretty cool!

But, ya know, before he became a 'Jesus follower', he was a tax collector. Tax collectors got a bad wrap back in the day. That's because they took people's hard-earned money and it was OK for them to do it. They could charge a person a little extra if they wanted to and stick it in their own pockets. A tax payer couldn't do or say anything about it. That stinks!

The Gospel of Matthew was written around A.D. 80 and begins with a little genealogy lesson on Jesus beginning with Abraham. It talks about Him as a human being (God sent to Earth in human form) and goes into detail of the things He did while He was here.

Matthew went on to become a great evangelist. He preached the Gospel in Hebrew to the Jewish folks for 15 years. Tradition tells us that he died a martyr around A.D. 100.

Mark

All we know about Mark is that he was a missionary traveling companion to three well-known fellas from the Bible: Paul, Peter and Barnabas. Based on what we learn from the Book of Acts, Mark was probably a young fella in-training and felt the calling to write down the story of Jesus. Records show that his version was written back around A.D. 55 and 65, which made him the first one to tell the story.

It could have been because Mark had some firsthand experiences walking with Jesus, but it's really unclear. However, some folks believe that Mark is mentioned as 'the young man that ran off naked when Jesus was arrested'. This would've made him the first documented 'streak' that the world has ever known. Ain't that neat?

And there followed him a certain young man, having a linen cloth cast about his naked body; and the young men laid hold on him: And he left the linen cloth, and fled from them naked. Mark 14: 51, 52

Mark was living in the Jerusalem area at the time and used his family's home for some of the early Christian meetings. This meant he basically used his house as a local church for folks to get together and talk about Jesus. And since 'being a Christian' in those days was up against so much opposition, having a home as a Christian church could have been dangerous. Doing something like this took courage.

Mark's version of the Gospel was originally written to the Roman Christians and provides many details of what Jesus did during His 'public' ministry – the miracles and teachings. Actually, the Book of Mark records more miracles than any of the other three Gospels. This meant Mark took great notes!

Tradition tells us that Mark died a martyr in Alexandria, Egypt around A.D. 68.

Luke

It is believed that Luke was Greek and a Gentile. He was born at Antioch in Syria. I personally don't have a clue where that is exactly, but I'm sure you have to cross an ocean to get there.

Luke was a doctor back in the day and must have been highly educated. I'm sure they wouldn't let just anybody do this kind of stuff. This probably called for scroll certificates that a person would have to earn at an accredited school or something. Luke was the real deal.

Luke, the beloved physician, and Demas, greet you. - Colossions 4: 14

In between surgeries and prescribing antibiotics, Luke found the time to write his Gospel and the Book of Acts. He must have been a busy man! Historic records tell us that this fella was never married and didn't have any kids. This would definitely give him more time to do other important things like hanging out with Apostle Paul doing ministry stuff.

Luke's Gospel was written around A.D. 60 and was sent to Theophilus and the Gentiles. It gives an accurate account of the life of Jesus and presents Him as the perfect human and Savior. It is considered the most comprehensive of all of the Gospels. That means it has a lot of details in there.

Catholic tradition tells us that Luke died at the ripe age of 84 of natural causes and that he lived a peaceful life.

John

John was one of the original twelve disciples. He began his life-long journey following Jesus when he was left with a choice of either to 'keep on fishin' for fish' or 'swap tackle and fish for men'. He chose the bigger catch.

John may have been a successful man because he was part of a family-owned fishing business. He and his brother, James (who was also a disciple of Jesus), worked together. Their job would have been to supply the town-folk with a variety of seafood and maybe they were distributors to the major restaurant chains of the day. Who knows? They would have had the duty of keeping their business floating in the competitive business world of fishing. They were businessmen. Then one day Jesus shows up and changes their world.

The Gospel of John was written sometime between A.D. 85 – 90. John's purpose was to prove to the world of believers and non-believers that Jesus was the Son of God. His Gospel doesn't include any genealogies, records of Jesus' birth, parables or even the Great Commission. It simply tells folks about Jesus and His free gift of eternal life for those that choose to believe in Him.

John is also given credit for writing other books of the Bible. Among his library credentials, it includes the following works:

Gospel of John I John
II John
III John
Revelation

John outlived all of the other twelve original disciples. The Bible doesn't tell us how or when he died. Some say he spent his retirement in Ephesus where he died at an old age around A.D. 100 of natural causes. He served the Lord to

13

the end.

Each of these men mentioned above had a major job to do by sharing the Gospel of Jesus Christ with the world. Their writings have become the proof we need that Jesus is who many of us believe He is. We, as Christians, have put our faith in Jesus because of the Gospel. We've heard it! We've read it! And now we believe it! Many of us are sharing it today because we know how truthful it is. We can see it in our changed lives and in the lives of others.

That's the basis of the four Gospel books from the Bible. It's to tell others about Jesus from all four sides of the box and gives them a little background about Him from different perspectives – Matthew, Mark, Luke and John. When we've heard the Gospel, we are all left with a decision of whether to believe it or not. It's our choice of what we want to do about it.

We could 'step up' and accept Jesus as our Lord and Savior and choose to follow Him. Or we could simply 'step back' and write the Gospel off as another fairy tale that sounds good around Christmas time.

What are you going to do about it?

The Beginning
John 1: 1-18

Before we can jump right in to the books of Matthew, Mark, Luke and John, we need to dig up some background information first. Stories of Jesus have been told for hundreds of years. Each of us probably already knows the basics. We may have seen the story on TV, at Sunday School, or even heard about Him from our grandparents.

When we think of Jesus, we paint a visual picture in our mind of a man that 'once upon a time' walked the Earth over 2000 years ago. We've seen several Jesus movies about

Him and figured that He probably had long hair, a neatly trimmed beard and a mustache. Right? Or maybe you've seen the 1970's hippie version that shows Jesus with a perm. He sorta looked like the Dad on The Brady Bunch. And what about those cool 'Jesus sandals? Don't forget about those.

We know from the stories that He chose twelve fellas to hang out with. They were pretty cool, except for the one fella that betrayed Him. What was his name? Judy's Carrot? Or something like that. He sold Jesus out for a bag of money. And how about that Peter fella? He was 'true blue through and through' until Jesus got arrested. He lied about knowing Jesus three times. And then out of the blue, a rooster starts crowing because Jesus said it would happen after his third lie. Peter was all freaking out and junk.

Anyway, the next thing you know, the Jewish people are whooping up on Jesus and eventually have Him killed. He dies on a cross with nails in his hands and feet. They even put a brier-lookin' thing on His head and mock Him by calling Him 'the King of Jews'. The story ends by Jesus dying and then He comes back to life for a little bit and then floats off to Heaven. The end.

It makes a great Easter story, don't it? I'm just not really sure what the egg-totin' bunny has to do with it. And why do they call him Peter Cottontail? I imagine it's all tied in there somewhere. Huh?

But when we start learning more about Jesus, we read that He was God in the flesh. He did a lot of cool stuff (like miracles) to prove to the world who He really was. His purpose for traveling so far from Heaven to Earth was to provide us with a solution to our 'sin problem'. He would take our burdens upon Himself and have them nailed to the cross. He was and is our ultimate sacrifice and our bridge to re-connect us with our Creator. All we have to do is believe in Him. You've heard all of this before, right?

Jesus – the Word

But, we can't start learning everything about His life just by looking at His Earthly arrival. It goes beyond that. According to John, He was there in the very beginning.

In the beginning was the Word, and the Word was with God, and the Word was God. The same was in the beginning with God. - John 1: 1, 2

And the Word was made flesh, and dwelt among us, (and we beheld his glory, the glory as of the only begotten of the Father,) full of grace and truth. - John 1: 14

John refers to Him as the Word and that He became flesh. But, a 'word' is usually what you would call something that has a bunch of letters bumped together, and when we say it, it sounds like something. You know what I'm saying? You would find a bunch of these 'words' in books and coming out of the mouths of folks that like to talk a lot.

Why would John call Jesus the 'Word'? What would that mean? Well, if you go back to the original Greek text of the Bible, you would see that 'Word' is translated from the Greek word "Logos" and it looks something like this:

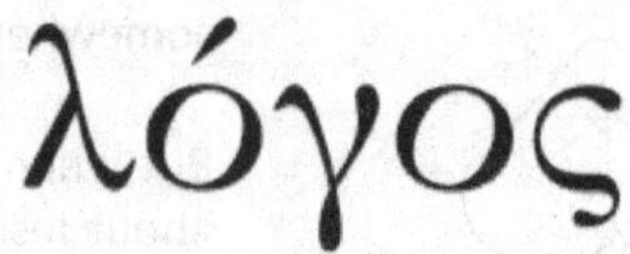

It basically means 'the cosmic mediator between God and the world' and 'the One that holds it all together' so to speak. It's a divine spiritual thing that our brains may have a hard time grabbing hold of. John is telling us that Jesus played a major role in the creation of the world, He is/was/and will forever be God and He's been there from the very beginning of time. We have to go passed the earthly Jesus mentality to understand His heavenly supreme awesomeness. You know what I mean?

He, as God, created everything. For some folks, we know about God (the Father), Jesus (God's Son) and the Holy Spirit (which is the presence of God in every believer). We may think of them as individual beings; each doing their own thing in the big universe. We may visualize the scenario into something worldly that we can relate to like a single Dad and his son.

But, God is made up of the Father, Son and Holy Spirit and each are the same God and are One. It's called the Trinity and it's a spiritual thing. The best illustration I have heard about how the Trinity works is described with water (H2O).

Water can be:
1) ice
2) a liquid
3) a vapor (steam)

But, yet they are all still water. You see what I saying?

There are many religions out there that don't believe Jesus is God. Some of them don't even believe He existed. I guess that's why John tells us:

He was in the world, and the world was made by him, and the world knew him not. - John 1: 10

Some folks are OK with believing in God as the Creator of the world, but they see Him as one person (one being). And then when Jesus is mentioned as God, it throws them for a loop. They think of Him from an Earthly view and see this fella trying to take credit for everything. They consider it blasphemous. They don't take into consideration all of the miracles, the prophecies about Him, and all of the proof He gave when He was here. Jesus is the Messiah, but folks didn't recognize Him.

Even today, Jews are still waiting for their promised Messiah. They believe that their Messiah will be a future King of Israel born of earthly parents in the blood line of King David. They will recognize him because there will be universal peace all over the world and things will be like they were back in the Old Testament days. This King will help them build their Third Temple. We all know him as the anti-

17

Christ which is mentioned in Revelation.

Sin?
Genesis 3: 1-19

Why did Jesus come to Earth in the first place? Great question.

It began a long time ago in the Garden of Eden when man and woman were created. Remember Adam and Eve? They were God's perfect creation and were living large in all that God created. Life was just peachy! They had direct access to everything and could eat anything they wanted. Well, except for that one fruit from the tree of knowledge that God warned them about. I mean, one tree among a bunch of them to choose from, I'm sure obeying God wouldn't have been a problem.

And then a serpent appeared on the scene. He was totally against

God's way of thinking. He tempted Adam and Eve and they gave in. They listened to Satan (the serpent) and disobeyed God by eating the forbidden fruit that He told them not to eat. This quick decision changed the course of all mankind forever.

Sin was created that day and has been the problem with humanity ever since. It's a problem because it goes against God. It's a serious thing regardless of what the world tells us. Sin separates us from Him. Actually,

God destroyed the world once already because of it. We learn this from the story of Noah and the Flood:

[Genesis 6: 1-8]

Remember that one? Noah was the only righteous person left on Earth, so God chose him and his family to start over with. One family out of all of the people on Earth? Wow! That's kinda sad.

But even after the flooding incident, the nature to 'go against God' came out of the ark that Noah built with the remaining survivors. The nature to sin was still in their blood and is still present in folks today. Everyone is included – even you. Yep!

Many years later, God set up a deal with a fella named Moses in the Old Testament that would help the people to remove their sin guilt and make them right in His eyes. This involved following a list of rules and codes to live by that He gave them personally. He wrote it on stone tablets so that it would last awhile.

[Exodus 20: 1 – 24: 4]

He also gave them instructions on how to worship Him and laws to help them live better with each other. It was a great plan and everybody agreed. They sealed the deal with the sprinkling of blood.

And Moses took the blood, and sprinkled it on the people, and said, Behold the blood of the covenant, which the LORD hath made with you concerning all these words. - Exodus 24: 8

The way things worked was that, if someone sinned, they would have to make sacrifices. This would temporarily remove the guilt of sin. This was a once a year thing and they called it The Day Of Atonement. This involved the shedding of the blood of bulls and goats.

For the life of the flesh is in the blood: and I have given it to you upon the altar to make an atonement for your souls: for it is the blood that maketh an atonement for the soul. - Leviticus 17: 11

It seems kinda gross and a little bit brutal, but this is how sin was atoned. But, ya know, it wasn't like they had a bloodfest and animals were laying dead all over the place with flies swarming around. They used them later for food and clothing just like we do today.

Folks like to say that sacrificing animals in the Old Testament was awful and downright terrible. But, it's really no different than today. Many of us don't even think about where our meat products come from. The food we eat comes from somewhere. Did you know that there are billions of animals slaughtered for that very purpose every year? The average American meateater is responsible for the death of over 2,000 chickens in their lifetime. Did you know that? We all like fried chicken, right?

As time passed, these folks weren't too focused on God. I'm sure they performed these yearly sacrifices out of obligation instead of being sincerely sorry for their sins. To them it may have been just another thing to do once a year like buying an anniversary card for our wife or something. And wives know if we are sincere about those cards, fellas.

Just sayin'.

I imagine they would be all shocked when the Day of Atonement date arrived. Maybe they accidentally checked their calendar and saw the occasion was coming up. They would frantically try to get everything together (sorta like we do with one of our kid's birthdays). If that wasn't enough stress, they had to remember all of the sins they committed that year, so that they would know what they were suppose to be sorry for.

"Honey, dd you make that sin list?"

"Yes, dear."

"Great. Hurry! Let's go get one of our pretty goats. The Day of Atonement's tomorrow. It sorta snuck up on us, didn't it?"

"Yes, dear."

It became more about obligation and duty, instead of being

sincerely sorry for sin.

Blood of Jesus
Hebrews 9: 11-28

We have heard of the blood of Jesus and may not realize it's great importance. By Him dying on the cross, He became the ultimate sacrifice for all humanity.

In the Old Testament, people would make their yearly sacrifice on the Day of Atonement. They would bring their unblemished animal and hand it over to the high priest. This fella would do his thing and be the middle guy between them and God. Of course, there was a process that had to be followed. It was a yearly event.

Jesus' death was similar to the Old Testament process, but it was a one time deal and actually removed sin to those that believe in Him. If it wasn't for Jesus and this New Covenant, everybody would still be killing goats.

The blood of Jesus saves us from spiritual death. He is our source of eternal life. He died so that we could live.

They Said He Would Come
God must have known there would be folks out there that would doubt Jesus as the Promised Messiah. Maybe that's why He had prophets back in the day to tell people about Him many years before He came.

Think about it. Let's say we were back in the old days and had never heard prophecies of a Messiah coming. Life was just your ordinary everyday thing. One day this fella walks up to us and says, "Hey ya'll! My name is Jesus and I created the world." We would probably laugh and think he was nuts.

However, if prophecies were told about His upcoming arrival and we were expecting Him, maybe this fella wouldn't be so

weird after all. Especially, if He started doing miracles and fulfilling the prophecies we were told about.

The Old Testament speaks of many prophecies about the Messiah before He came. From them, we can see that Jesus is who He says He is. Here are some of them:

1. The Messiah was to be born in Bethlehem.
• OT Prophecy: Micah 5: 2
• NT Fulfillment: Matthew 2: 1-6, Luke 2: 1-20

2. The Messiah was to be born of a virgin.
- OT Prophecy: Isaiah 7: 14
- NT Fulfillment: Matthew 1: 18-25, Luke 1: 26-38

3. The Messiah was to be a prophet like Moses.
- OT Prophecy: Deuteronomy 18: 15, 18, 19
- NT Fulfillment: John 7: 40

4. The Messiah was to enter Jerusalem in triumph.
- OT Prophecy: Zechariah 9: 9
- NT Fulfillment: Matthew 21: 1-9, John 12: 12-16

5. The Messiah was to be rejected by His own people.
- OT Prophecy: Isaiah 53: 1, 3, Psalm 118: 22
- NT Fulfillment: Matthew 26: 14-16, John 12: 37-43, Acts: 4: 1-12

6. The Messiah was to be betrayed by one of His followers.
- OT Prophecy: Psalm 41: 9
- NT Fulfillment: Matthew 26: 14-16, 47-50, Luke 22: 19-23

7. The Messiah was to be tried and condemned.
- OT Prophecy: Isaiah 53: 8
- NT Fulfillment: Luke 23: 1-25, Matthew 27: 1, 2

8. The Messiah was to be silent before His accusers.
- OT Prophecy: Isaiah 53: 7
- NT Fulfillment: Matthew 27: 12-14, Mark: 15: 3, 4, Luke 23: 8-10

9. The Messiah was to be struck and spit on by His enemies.
- OT Prophecy: Isaiah 50: 6
- NT Fulfillment: Matthew 26: 67, 27: 30, Mark 14: 65

10. The Messiah was to be mocked and insulted.
- OT Prophecy: Psalm 22: 7, 8
- NT Fulfillment: Matthew 27: 39-44, Luke 23: 11, 35

11. The Messiah was to die by crucifixion.
- OT Prophecy: Psalm 22: 14, 16, 17
- NT Fulfillment: Matthew 27: 31, Mark 15: 20, 25

12. The Messiah was to suffer with criminals and pray for His enemies.
- OT Prophecy: Isaiah 53: 12
- NT Fulfillment: Matthew 27: 38, Mark 15: 27, 28, Luke 23: 32-34

13. The Messiah was to be given vinegar and gall.
- OT Prophecy: Psalm 69: 21
- NT Fulfillment: Matthew 27: 34, John 19: 28-30

14. Others were to cast lots for the Messiah's garments.
- OT Prophecy: Psalm 22: 18
- NT Fulfillment: John 19: 23, 24

15. The Messiah's bones were not to be broken.
- OT Prophecy: Exodus 12: 46

• NT Fulfillment: John 19: 31-36

16. The Messiah was to die as a sacrifice for sin.

• OT Prophecy: Isaiah 53: 5, 6, 8, 10, 11, 12

• NT Fulfillment: John 1: 29; 11: 49-52, Acts 10: 43; 13: 38, 39

17. The Messiah was to be raised from the dead.

• OT Prophecy: Psalm 16: 10

• NT Fulfillment: Acts 2: 22-32, Matthew 28: 1-10

18. The Messiah is now at God's right hand.

• OT Prophecy: Psalm 110: 1

• NT Fulfillment: Mark 16: 19, Luke 24: 50, 51

Jesus fulfilled the prophecies of long ago as we can clearly see. The Gospels contain all of the historic information we need to know about Him. Since we know about sin and how it separates us from God, we can now understand how important Jesus is to the salvation of the world.

This makes the birth of Jesus something special that we can all celebrate. Our Messiah has come – the Promised Savior of the world. Yay!

Like I said before, the Books of Matthew, Mark, Luke and John give a bunch of details about Jesus. It tells us about His birth, His parents, His early ministry, His disciples and followers, His teachings and miracles, the many times He is persecuted, His death and resurrection, and many others things. It's kinda hard for me to write it all down and explain it without creating several books that resemble the encyclopedia collection that our parents would buy us when we were younger.

Instead, I've chosen to include a chronological time line that refers you to the scriptures. This is for your benefit so that you can look them up in your Bible and study them. I encourage you to do it. You might learn a thing or two.

On occasion, I might write a little something I found interesting and may add my two cents. You should still go back and check out those scriptures. We're talking about Jesus and knowing more about His life will only make us wiser and better followers. You know what I'm saying?

The Birth and Early Childhood of Christ

Subject	Matthew	Mark	Luke	John
Birth of John Baptist foretold			1:5-25	
Annunciation of the birth of Jesus			1:26-38	
Mary visits Elizabeth			1:39-56	
Birth of John the Baptist			1:57-80	
The two genealogies	1:1-17		3:23-38	
Birth of Jesus Christ	1:18-25		2:1-7	
The watching shepherds			2:8-20	
The circumcision			2:21	
Presentation in the temple			2:22-38	
The wise men from the East	2:1-12			
Flight into Egypt, and return to Nazareth	2:13-23		2:39	
Christ in the temple with the doctors			2:40-52	

The Christmas Story

Gabriel Talks To Mary
Luke 1: 26-38

In the sixth month, God sends an angel (Gabriel) down to Nazareth to speak to a virgin woman who was pledged to marry a fella named Joseph. These were ordinary folks, probably poor or lower class, but God saw something in this woman and chose to use her for something great. Her name was Mary and would be the mother of Jesus. That's a big deal! Gabriel gives her some insight into God's master plan that included her into the picture.

Mary is scared and probably all excited. However, she was a little confused. How in the world would she have a kid if she was still a virgin? That's simple — it's called spiritual insemination. Basically, gettin' pregnant without having sex. Don't worry. This has only happened once. And she was cool with it.

Within a six month period, God had already began working. He needed someone to give a future introduction to Jesus, so he allowed one of Mary's kinfolk to have a baby named John. He was later called John the Baptist because he baptized folks with water. He told people about Jesus and gave them a 'heads up' before He entered the scene.

An Angel Talks To Joseph
Matthew 1: 18-25

Joseph was Mary's future husband. They weren't married yet, but were planning on it. I'm sure they were all excited about it and made all the wedding invitations and stuff. Joseph might have had a place picked out for them and made things ready. But, there was this one little problem. Mary was pregnant and Joseph knew it wasn't his. Uh oh!

Joseph believed her story about the 'spiritual insemination' thing, but he was a righteous man and loved her. He didn't want folks to be pointing fingers at her for being pregnant before marriage and have her go through being disgraced out in public. He decided to call things off in a quiet and peaceful manner.

But before he made his final decision, an angel of the Lord came down to him in a dream. The angel told him to go on ahead and follow through with the marriage. God knew about it and that Joseph shouldn't worry. It was all good and part of the plan that was prophesied in the days of old.

[Isaiah 7: 14]

The angel even helped him pick out a great name to call his new son. He was to call him Jesus (which means 'the Lord saves'). Folks will also know Him as Immanuel (which means 'God with us').

Joseph went ahead and done what the angel told him to do. He married Mary. However, they didn't join together until after she gave birth. This was probably nine months later.

Jesus Is Born In Bethlehem

Luke 2: 1-7

The prophets of the Old Testament said that the Messiah would be born in a town called Bethlehem. Well, unfortunately Joseph and Mary both lived in Nazareth. If Jesus were born in Nazareth, then the prophesy about Him being the Messiah wouldn't hold water. You know what I mean? But, God had that all worked out.

Back in those days, Caesar Augustus issued a decree that a census should be done on all of the folks living in the Roman world. This means he wanted a head count. This was probably so that he would know who lived there for military purposes or maybe so that he could charge them taxes. Since Joseph was an honest man, he packed his bags and took Mary with him on their journey to Bethlehem to fill out the proper paperwork. Keep in mind, Mary was pregnant. I imagine she was miserable the whole trip.

Here we have a couple making a road trip. This was around 70 miles and could have taken them days to get there. If the bumpy camel ride wasn't enough discomfort, Mary was also having contractions. She finally gave birth in the city limits of Bethlehem. Prophesy fulfilled! Unfortunately, all the hotels were booked up because everybody in the Roman world was already there filling out census paperwork. What were Mary and Joseph to do?

All they could do was deliver the baby themselves, wrap Him up in some clothes and place Him in the most convenient area at the time – an animal feeding trough (called a manger). You've heard that word before, right?

Shepherds Visit Jesus
Luke 2: 8-20

It was night time and, there in the open fields, a few shepherds were watching over their flock like all good shepherds did back in the day. All of a sudden, an angel appears right before their eyes. I imagine it was kinda bright and scary. It may have freaked them out a bit.

The angel tells them to not be afraid because they had some good news to tell them and all the world.

"Today, in the city of David, a Savior is born."

At that moment, the sky was filled with heavenly hosts and they all began praising God. I bet this was the best light show they had ever seen in the sky. Fireworks weren't invented back then, so this may have been the first time anything like this had ever happened.

The shepherds packed their bags and headed out to Bethlehem. They remembered the tip that the angel gave about how and where to find Him, so they were set as they traveled on. When they got there, they found Mary, Joseph and baby Jesus just like the angel had said. They immediately spread the news and it spread like wild fire.

Mary And Joseph Visit The Temple

Luke 2: 21-40

According to Jewish customs, there were three things that had to be done when a baby was born:

Circumcision – This was performed on all Jewish baby boys when they were eight days old. This was to show their separation from the Gentile folks and their special relationship with God. They were also named on the eighth day. That's kinda weird because what would folks call your newborn son during the first seven days? Boy? Young fella?

Redemption of the first born – A firstborn son was presented to God one month after his birth. The ceremony included redeeming him (buying him back) from God through an offering. Parents back then realized that their child belonged to God.

Purification of the mother – When a woman gives birth to a child, she is considered ceremonially unclean. This means she can't enter the temple. She would have to wait 40 days after giving birth to a son and 80 days for a girl. I guess having girls makes you yuckier. After the waiting period, she could bring an offering of a lamb, dove or pigeon to the high priest and he would clean her up.

Mary and Joseph did everything by the book (according to God's Law). This meant that Jesus wasn't born above the law, but instead, He came to fulfill it. They met a righteous man named Simeon who was told by the Holy Spirit that he would not die until he saw Jesus. He spoke some words about Him that may have came as a shock. He said that Jesus was a gift from God and that He was the Messiah that would bring light to the world for both Jews and Gentiles. This would be both good news and bad news for the folks in Israel because many of them would reject Him. Can you imagine the feeling Mary had knowing that there would be people out there that wouldn't like her new baby boy? Mamas tend to take that kind of stuff personally. Ya know? I know a few that would 'body slam' you for saying something bad about their kid. I guess Mary had to learn to count to ten a lot and turn the other cheek a bunch.

They also met an old prophetess named Anna. She was a dedicated temple-goer. It says she never left. Sounds like some church members I know. It says she would pray and fast a lot, too. I imagine she was highly respected as a righteous woman among the temple crowd. She thanked God for the birth of Jesus and shared some words about Him to the folks looking for the redemption of Jerusalem. This was like putting a 'stamp of approval' from someone that people trusted religiously.

After Joseph and Mary did everything that was required of them according to the Law of the Lord, they headed out toward their hometown of Nazareth. Jesus continued to grow and became strong with wisdom. It says that God's grace was on Him.

There is a gap of a few years from the time they left Bethlehem and went back to Nazareth. The upcoming verses from Matthew will help us to tie in those loose ends.

Jesus Gets Visitors From The East
Matthew 2: 1-12

We have always been taught

from a Christmas song that 'three wise men from the Orient are... bearings gifts and they traveled so far', but here we read that it simply says 'wise men' and no one counted how many there were. And just because they came from the East, does that make them Chinese? That's almost racial profiling, ain't it?

Tradition says that these smart fellas came from a place called Parthia, which would've been thousands of miles away making this a major road trip.

From these verses we see that these wise men followed a star that led them to where Jesus was in Bethlehem. Not much is known about this 'star' except that the wise men saw it. No one saw this thing other than them. It could have been a special celestial light from God that only they could see. I personally wouldn't recommend following stars to get you anywhere because they might get you lost. Star-following wouldn't be good for long journeys because they fade away when daylight comes. And then what? You would be stuck in the middle of nowhere. God was definitely in charge of this journey because He got them to their destination.

When they found baby Jesus, they worshiped Him and brought Him some gifts: gold, frankincense and myrrh. That sounds like some awesome gifts for a baby and were probably expensive. All my kids got was diapers, noise makers, and butt wipes. The gifts that the wise men brought were special and had spiritual meaning.

- **Gold – a gift for royalty**
- **Frankincense – a gift for deity**
- **Myrrh – a spice for someone that was going to die.**

These expensive gifts were probably used by Mary and Joseph to help them cover their traveling expenses.

When the wise men saw the star, they came to Jerusalem. They spoke with the king at the time and asked him if he knew where this 'king of the Jews' was born. This king at the time was King Herod the Great and their question probably came as a shock. He felt that someone was about to overtake his throne and invade his 'king space'. Based on old prophecies, he knew that a ruler was to be born in Bethlehem one day. Now that day had come. What was he going to do?

King Herod worked a deal with the wise men and told them to let him know when they found this special kid. He wanted to worship Him, too. This was really a lie because his purpose to have Him killed. He didn't want someone taking over his throne and messing up his playhouse.

The wise men eventually found baby Jesus, but felt kinda funny about going back and telling King Herod about it. They received a warning in a dream and decided to return home through another route. The King's plan was ruined.

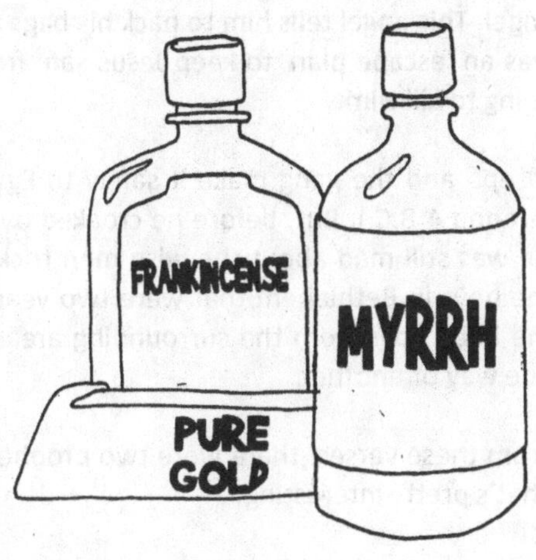

The Escape To Egypt
Matthew 2: 1-18

Joseph gets a dream from an

angel. This angel tells him to pack his bags and take Mary and Jesus to Egypt. It was an 'escape plan' to keep Jesus safe from King Herod. This crazy fella was going to kill Him.

Joseph and the gang make it safely to Egypt and stay there until Herod dies (around 4 B.C.). But, before he croaked over, he did something totally insane. He was still mad about the wise men tricking him, so he decided to kill all of the boys in Bethlehem that were two years old and under. This also included the baby boys from the surrounding areas. He was determined to find Jesus one way or another.

From these verses, there were two prophecies about Jesus that were fulfilled. That's pretty interesting.

The Return To Nazareth
Matthew 2: 19-23

Joseph receives another grand appearance from an angel in a dream. The angel tells him to get his stuff together and move his family to Israel. King Herod and some of the other folks, that wanted Jesus killed, had died. It was safe for them to move on. So, Joseph did. When Joseph found out that Herod's son was the ruler in Judea, he was afraid of what could happen. The warning he received in a dream made him decide to take another route and move to Nazareth. This was their hometown. It seems their journey brought them full circle back to where they had started. But, Jesus was safe and that's all that mattered.

Another prophecy was fulfilled. Jesus will be called a Nazarene.

Jesus As A Kid

Luke 2: 41-52

This may be the only account of Jesus as a pre-teen. The verses tell us that He was 12 years old and He's found here hanging out with a group of teachers at the temple in Jerusalem. What was He doing there?

According to God's Law, every male was required to go to Jerusalem three times a year for some awesomely cool festivals:

Three times in a year shall all thy males appear before the LORD thy God in the place which he shall choose; in the feast of unleavened bread, and in the feast of weeks, and in the feast of tabernacles: and they shall not appear before the LORD empty: - Deuteronomy 16: 16

Feast of Unleavened Bread (Passover - Pesach)
Feast of Weeks (Shavuot)
Feast of Tabernacles (Sukkot)

According to the verses, Jesus and His earthly family was in Jerusalem celebrating the Feast of the Passover which would've been some time between March and April. This festival would have lasted about seven to eight days. When it was over, Joseph and Mary packed up their stuff and headed back home. Unfortunately, they forgot to pack a very important item. They forgot Jesus. They accidentally left Him behind and didn't recognize that He was missing until a whole day of traveling. I'm just glad DFACS wasn't invented yet because they would have been up against some serious charges. I think it would be called 'reckless abandonment' or something.

They went back to Jerusalem and found Jesus three days later hanging out with a group of teachers from the temple. I have a feeling that Jesus got scolded by his Mom. I'm sure she was worried. I also feel that she may have been amazed at how smart He had become when it came to religious stuff. Even the teachers were fascinated with how much He knew.

Did Jesus Have Brothers And Sisters?
Matthew 13: 55, 56
Mark 6: 3

I have always had the impression that Jesus was an only child. That meant that He didn't have brothers or sisters. But, as I dig deeper into the scriptures, I see that He wasn't alone in the family. Joseph and Mary had other kids.

Yes, she was a virgin when Jesus was born. After that, it sounds like Joseph and Mary kept breeding. According to the verses, He had sisters (more than one) and four brothers. Unfortunately, the Bible only gives us the names of the brothers:

James
Joses
Simon
Judas

This tells me that Jesus didn't grow up all by Himself. He had brothers and sisters to play with and talk to. I'm sure they all did normal things that brothers and sisters do today. They may have fussed and fought and even had great times together. Bonds were probably created. This could have helped Him develop personable social skills that He could use later in ministry.

His Earthly Dad Was A Carpenter?
Matthew 13: 55, 56
Mark 6: 3

People knew Joseph as a carpenter. This was his occupation and career. He could've had a family business that involved building stuff for people to make money. The poor fella had a bunch of mouths to feed and carpentry work was his way to do it.

If it were a family business, then the smart thing would be for him to use the valuable resources he had around him to help his business succeed.

This would include the free labor that his family offered. He had daughters and five boys that could help carry their load in the home. I'm sure they all took part in the business.

Joseph could also teach his kids the valuable lessons of hard work, respecting authority, accomplishing goals, and all the other stuff that can be learned from having a Dad as your boss. A lot of family values going on right here! Another important thing would be the example they were making to others of how a family should work together as a team. That's good stuff right there!

John The Baptist
Luke 1: 5-25

John the Baptist and Jesus were pretty close to the same age (roughly 6 months difference). John was a special kid because he was an answered prayer to an old couple named Zechariah and Elizabeth.

Zechariah was a priest that belonged to the priestly division of Abijah. His wife, Elizabeth, was a descendant of Aaron, who was also another priest. I get the feeling that these two people were all 'priestly' and junk because the verses say that both of them had it going on in God's eyes. That meant He was happy of how they turned out.

They were both up in age and never had any children. This was a sad thing because, according to Jewish beliefs, children were a blessing because they added value to a family's social and financial status. Keep in mind, everybody in a family worked together back then. Kids didn't leave it all up to parents to do all the work while they sat around all day playing video games. They chipped in, too. Plus, as parents got older, kids would take care of them. Zechariah and Elizabeth weren't blessed in this area, so maybe the Jews looked down on them as if they were being cursed with a plague. It was like they had 'social cooties' or something.

One day Zechariah gets a visitor while he worked at the temple doing what all cool priests did back in the day. An angel shows up and tells him, "Hey! My name is Gabriel and guess what? You're going to have a baby boy. You will call him John."

Zechariah didn't believe a word of it. This later resulted in nine months of not being able to speak. It was only until Elizabeth delivered the baby that Zechariah could say a word. Until then, he was totally speechless. He may have learned a valuable lesson, like not doubting angels when they tell you stuff. Sometimes it's best to just agree and move on.

John Prepares The Way For Jesus
Matthew 3: 1-12
Mark 1: 1-8
Luke 3: 1-18

John the Baptist must have been a rough looking fella. You would think that since he came from a bloodline of priests that he would at least look like one. I mean, come on! His clothes were made from camel hair? He ate grasshoppers and honey? Yuck! He was a mess!

However, he was the prophet that was prophesied about many years before from Isaiah. The voice of him that crieth in the wilderness, Prepare ye the way of the LORD, make straight in the desert a highway for our God.
- Isaiah 40: 3

John was the real deal! His God-given purpose was to preach about Jesus – to prepare the way. He told them about sin and how they all needed forgiveness. He baptized folks with water and people from all over Jordan and Jerusalem would come see him.

Even Jesus paid him a visit.

The Baptism of Christ				
Subject	Matthew	Mark	Luke	John
Ministry of John the Baptist	3:1-12	1:1-8	3:1-18	1:15-31
Baptism of Jesus Christ	3:13-17	1:9-11	3:21, 22	1:32-34

John was doing his thing at the Jordan River – ya know, baptizing folks, preaching and stuff. Standing there in line waiting His turn was Jesus. He had came from Galilee and probably walked the entire distance. Church buses weren't invented yet.

John recognizes Jesus among the crowd. He knew this fella was someone special and that He was the One that he had been preaching about the whole time. When it came time for him to baptize Jesus, John hesitated because he felt unworthy.

"I need to be baptized by you. Why would you come to me?' John tells Him.

John baptizes Him anyway, and as soon as he does, Heaven opens up and he sees the Spirit of God. It descended on Him like a dove. It may have been a strange but great feeling. After that, he then hears a voice from Heaven say, "This is my beloved Son, in whom I am well pleased."

We later learn from the Gospels that John the Baptist dies a terrible death. He is beheaded by King Herod the Tetrarch (who was the son of King Herod the Great) as part of a promise he made to a dancing girl's mother (Herodias).

[Matthew 14: 1-12, Mark 6: 14-29 and Luke 9: 7-9]

The Temptation of Christ				
Subject	Matthew	Mark	Luke	John
The temptation	4:1-11	1:12, 13	4:1-13	

Jesus Is Tempted

Matthew 4: 1-11
Mark 1: 12, 13
Luke 4: 1-13

Immediately after Jesus' baptism, He is led by the Spirit into the desert to be tempted by the devil. That's when the 'tempter' started working on Him pretty hard. The interesting thing to me is that the devil used real 'needs' to test Him with: physical needs, emotional needs and psychological needs.

Temptation #1 (Physical)

Jesus was already hungry from all that fasting he had done. He had went without food for forty days and forty nights. This was the same thing that Moses and Elijah did in the Old Testament when they wanted to focus more on God and not the cravings of the flesh.

And he was there with the LORD forty days and forty nights; he did neither eat bread, nor drink water. And he wrote upon the tables the words of the covenant, the ten commandments. Exodus 34: 28

40

And the angel of the LORD came again the second time, and touched him, and said, Arise and eat; because the journey is too great for thee. And he arose, and did eat and drink, and went in the strength of that meat forty days and forty nights unto Horeb the mount of God. - 1 Kings 19: 7, 8

The devil begins tempting Jesus by saying, "If you're the Son of God, turn these stones into bread."

But he answered and said, *It is written, Man shall not live by bread alone, but by every word that proceedeth out of the mouth of God. - Matthew 4: 4*

Jesus was fasting so that He could focus more on spiritual stuff. The devil came along to try and distract Him by tempting Him to focus more on His physical needs. Jesus knew the importance of spiritual nourishment and won the battle with the use of scripture.

Temptation #2 (Emotional)
The devil takes Jesus to the holy city and has Him stand on the highest part of the temple. He tells Him, "If you're the Son of God, throw yourself down."

Jesus said unto him, It is written again, Thou shalt not tempt the Lord thy God. - Matthew 4: 7

This temptation had more to do with trusting God in all situations.

"Would He take care of me?"
"Does He love me enough to help me?"

Jesus knew that He would always be there for Him. He also knew that you don't put God to foolish tests like hanging off of a ledge and jumping to see if He would catch you. That's just insane! Jesus beat this temptation with the use of scripture.

Temptation #3 (Psychological)

The devil takes Him to a very high mountain and shows Him all the kingdoms of the world. He says, "I'll give you all of this if you will bow down and worship me."

Then saith Jesus unto him, Get thee hence, Satan: for it is written, Thou shalt worship the Lord thy God, and him only shalt thou serve. - Matthew 4: 10

This temptation attacked the human's desire to want stuff; to be financially secure and to have the finer things of life. It's also about pride of wanting everything to be 'all about me'. Jesus used scripture again to beat this temptation. He knew that God was number one priority over all things.

These are the same things that we are all tempted with by the devil. We should follow Jesus' example and fight back. When we're tempted, use God's Word as a sword to defeat the enemy.

The Early Ministry of Christ				
Subject	Matthew	Mark	Luke	John
Andrew and another disciple and Simon Peter				1:35-42
Philip and Nathanael				1:43-51
The marriage in Cana of Galilee				2:1-11
Passover and cleansing the temple				2:12-25
Nicodemus comes to Jesus by night				3:1-21
Christ and John baptizing				3:22; 4:2
Christ at the well of Sychar				4:3-42
John the Baptist in prison	4:12; 14:3	1:14; 4:17	3:19, 20	3:24
Christ returns to Galilee	4:12	1:14, 15	4:14, 15	4:43-45
The synagogue at Nazareth			4:16-30	

Jesus' Ministry Begins

Luke 4: 14, 15

After Jesus got baptized, His ministry officially began. The year was around 27 – 29 A.D and He was about 30 years old (according to Luke 3: 23). He was geared up spiritually and ready to go.

[Matthew 4: 18-22, Mark 1: 16-20, Luke 5: 1-20]

His first preaching service started around the area of Galilee. While He was there, He invites His first two disciples (Peter and Andrew) to join Him on His journey. Andrew was already a disciple of John the Baptist, but was amazed at Jesus and decided to follow Him. He gets his brother, Peter, to come along, too.

There on the sea of Galilee, Jesus sees two fishermen mending their nets. They were hanging out in a boat with their Dad, Zebedee, in their family-owned fishing business. Jesus gives them the invitation. Immediately, James and John decide to jump ship and join the gang.

At this point, Jesus is making His rounds in the area. He's healing folks, preaching, and doing some totally awesome miracles. Lives are being changed and folks are starting to take notice. This includes the Jewish group of religious folks that weren't too impressed with what He was doing. Throughout Jesus' ministry, they look for reasons to accuse Him of breaking the rules and create a lot of trouble.

[Matthew 9: 9; Mark 2: 13, 14; Luke 5: 27, 28]

Matthew joins the group and invites everybody to his house for dinner. Not only are Jesus and His disciples there, but there are others. It's a wide variety of tax collectors, religious leaders, and regular folk (Luke 5: 29-32). During this scene, Jesus is questioned about why He hangs out with sinners. His response?

"I came not to call the righteous, but sinners to repentance." - Luke 5: 32

This was the mission of Jesus. He wanted folks to realize they were lost in their sins and needed forgiveness. Instead of sacrificing animals once a year with a heartless attitude, they could now receive forgiveness through Him. He would be the ultimate sacrifice for the sins of the world.

The number of disciples and followers continued to grow as Jesus made His evangelistic tour. Added to the disciple roster were:

Peter
Andrew
James the Greater
James the Lesser
John
Philip
Bartholomew
Matthew
Thomas
Thaddeus
Simon
Judas Iscariot
Matthias (Judas Iscariot's replacement as the 12th disciple)

Miracles of Christ

Subject	Matthew	Mark	Luke	John
The nobleman's son at Capernaum healed				4:46-54
The demoniac in the synagogue healed		1:21-28	4:31-37	
Simon's wife's mother healed	8:14-17	1:29-34	4:38-41	
Circuit round Galilee	4:23-25	1:35-39	4:42-44	
Healing a leper	8:1-4	1:40-45	5:12-16	
Christ stills the storm	8:18-27	4:35-41	8:22-25	
Demoniacs in the land of the Gadarenes	8:28-34	5:1-20	8:26-39	
Jairus' daughter. Woman healed	9:18-26	5:21-43	8:40-56	
Blind men and demoniac	9:27-34			
Healing the paralytic	9:1-8	2:1-12	5:17-26	
Matthew the publican	9:9-13	2:13-17	5:27-32	
"Thy disciples fast not"	9:14-17	2:18-22	5:33-39	

The Feast and Miracle at Bethesda

Subject	Matthew	Mark	Luke	John
The feast at Jerusalem				5:1
The pool of Bethesda				5:2-15
Jesus and the irate Jews				5:16-47

Ministry and Parables

Subject	Matthew	Mark	Luke	John
Plucking ears of corn on the Sabbath	12:1-8	2:23-28	6:1-5	
The withered hand. Miracles	12:9-21	3:1-12	6:6-11	
The twelve apostles	10:2-4	3:13-19	6:12-16	
The sermon on the mount	5:1-7:29		6:17-49	
The centurion's servant healed	8:5-13		7:1-10	
The widow's son at Nain			7:11-17	
Messengers from john	11:2-19		7:18-35	
Woe denounced to the cities of Galilee	11:20-24			
Call to the meek and suffering	11:25-30			
Anointing the feet of Jesus			7:36-50	
Second circuit round Galilee			8:1-3	
Parable of the sower	13:1-23	4:1-20	8:4-15	
Parable of the candle under a bushel		4:21-25	8:16-18	

Subject	Matthew	Mark	Luke	John
Parable of the seed growing secretly		4:26-29		
Parable of the wheat and tares	13:24-30			
Parable of the grain of mustard seed	13:31, 32	4:30-32	13:18, 19	
Parable of the leaven	13:33		13:20, 21	
On teaching by parables	13:34, 35	4:33-34		
The wheat and tares explained	13:36-43			
The hid treasure, the pearl, the net	13:44-52			
His mother and His brethren	12:46-50	3:31-35	8:19-21	
Reception at Nazareth	13:53-58	6:1-6		
Third circuit round Galilee	9:35-38; 11:1	6:6		
Sending forth of the twelve	10:5-42	6:7-13	9:1-6	
Herod's opinion of Jesus	14:1, 2	6:14-16	9:7-9	
Death of John the Baptist	14:3-12	6:17-29		
Feeding of the five thousand	14:13-21	6:30-44	9:10-17	6:1-15
Christ walking on the sea	14:22-33	6:45-52		6:16-21
Miracles in Gennesaret	14:34-36	6:53-56		
"The bread of life"				6:22-65
The washed hands	15:1-20	7:1-23		
The Syrophoenician woman	15:21-28	7:24-30		
Miracles of healing	15:29-31	7:31-37		
Feeding of the four thousand	15:32-39	8:1-9		
The sign from heaven	16:1-4	8:10-13		
The leaven of the Pharisees	16:5-12	8:14-21		
Blind man healed		8:22-26		

Outside of Galilee

Subject	Matthew	Mark	Luke	John
Peter's profession of faith	16:13-19	8:27-29	9:18-20	6:66-71
The passion foretold	16:20-28	8:30-9:1	9:21-27	
The transfiguration	17:1-9	9:2-10	9:28-36	
The coming of Elias	17:10-13	9:11-13		
The lunatic healed	17:14-21	9:14-29	9:37-42	

Back in Galilee

Subject	Matthew	Mark	Luke	John
The passion again foretold	17:22, 23	9:30-32	9:43-45	
The fish caught for the tribute	17:24-27			
The little child	18:1-5	9:33-37	9:46-48	
One casting out devils		9:38-41	9:49, 50	

Subject	Matthew	Mark	Luke	John
Offenses	18:6-9	9:42-48	17:2	
The lost sheep	18:10-14		15:4-7	
Forgiveness of injuries	18:15-17			
"Binding and loosing"	18:18-20			
Parable of the unmerciful servant	18:21-35			
"Salt with fire"		9:49, 50		

Ministry in Jerusalem

Subject	Matthew	Mark	Luke	John
Journey to Jerusalem			9:51	7:1-10
Fire from heaven			9:52-56	
Answers to disciples	8:19-22		9:57-62	
Teaching at the feast of tabernacles				7:11-53
Woman taken in adultery				8:1-11
Dispute with the Pharisees				8:12-59
The man born blind				9:1-41
The good shepherd				10:1-21
Feast of the dedication				10:22-30
Departure beyond Jordan				10:40-42

In Galilee

Subject	Matthew	Mark	Luke	John
Mission of the seventy			10:1-16	
The return of the seventy			10:17-24	
The good Samaritan			10:25-37	
Mary and Martha			10:38-42	
The Lord's prayer	6:9-13		11:1-4	
Prayer effectual	7:7-11		11:5-13	
The blasphemous Pharisees reproved	12:22-37	3:20-30	11:14-23	
The unclean spirit returning	12:43-45		11:24-28	
The sign of Jonah	12:38-42		11:29-32	
The light of the body	5:15; 6:22, 23		11:33-36	
The Pharisees	23:1-39		11:37-54	
What to fear	10:26-33		12:1-12	
Covetousness	6:25, 33		12:13-31	
Watchfulness			11:32-54	
Galileans that perished			13:1-9	

Subject	Matthew	Mark	Luke	John
Woman healed on the Sabbath			13:10-17	
The grain of mustard-seed	13:31, 32	4:30-32	13:18, 19	
The leaven		13:33	13:20, 21	

Towards and At Jerusalem

Subject	Matthew	Mark	Luke	John
Journey towards Jerusalem			13:22	
"Are there few that be saved?"			13:23-30	
Warning against Herod			13:31-33	
Prophecy against Jerusalem	23:37-39		13:34, 35	
Dropsy healed on the Sabbath day			14:1-6	
Choosing the chief rooms			14:7-14	
Parable of the great supper	22:1-14		14:15-24	
Following Christ with the cross	10:37, 38		14:25-35	
Parables of the lost sheep, piece of money, prodigal son			15:1-32	
Parables of the steward, rich man and Lazarus			16:1-31	
Offenses	18:6-15		17:1-4	
Faith and merit	17:20		17:5-10	
The ten lepers			17:11-19	
How the kingdom cometh			17:20-37	
Parable of the unjust judge			18:1-8	
Parable of the Pharisee and the publican			18:9-14	
Divorce	19:1-12	10:1-12		
Infants brought to Jesus	19:13-15	10:13-16	18:15-17	
The rich man inquiring	19:16-26	10:17-27	18:18-27	
Promises to the disciples	19:27-30	10:28-31	18:28-30	
Laborers in the vineyard	20:1-16			
Death of Christ foretold	20:17-19	10:32-34	18:31-34	
Request of James and John	20:20-28	10:35-45		
Blind men at Jericho	20:29-34	10:46-52	18:35-43	
Zaccheus			19:1-10	
Parable of the ten talents	25:14-30		19:11-28	
Raising of Lazarus				11:1-44
Meeting of the Sanhedrin				11:45-53
Christ Departs to Ephraim				11:54-57
The anointing by Mary	26:6-13	14:3-9	7:36-50	12:1-11
Christ enters Jerusalem	21:1-11	11:1-10	19:29-44	12:12-

Cleansing the temple (second)	21:12-16	11:15-18	19:45-48	
The barren fig tree	21:17-22	11:11-14, 11:19-23		
Exhortation to prayer and forgiveness	6:14-15	11:24-26		
The questioning of the chief priests	21:23-27	11:27-33	20:1-8	
Parable of the two sons	21:28-32			
Parable of the wicked husbandmen	21:33-46	12:1-12	20:9-18	
Parable of the wedding-garment	22:1-14		14:16-24	
The tribute money	22:15-22	12:13-17	20:20-26	
The Sadducees confuted	22:23-33	12:18-27	20:27-40	
The great commandment	22:34-40	12:28-34		
David's Son and David's Lord	22:41-46	12:35-37	20:41-44	
The hypocrisy and ambition of the Pharisees	23:1-39	12:38-40	20:45-47	
The widow's mite		12:41-44	21:1-4	
Christ's second coming foretold	24:1-51	13:1-37	21:5-36	
Parable of the ten virgins	25:1-13			
Parable of the talents	25:14-30		19:11-27	
The last judgment	25:31-46			
Greeks visit Jesus. Voice from heaven				12:20-36
The judgment of unbelief				12:37-50
Last passover. Conspiracy of Jews	26:1-5	14:1, 2	22:1, 2	
Judas Iscariot	26:14-16	14:10, 11	22:3-6	
Paschal supper	26:17-30	14:12-26	22:7-23	13:1-35
Contention of the apostles			22:24-30	
Peter's fall foretold	26:31-35	14:27-31	22:31-39	13:36-38
Last discourse. The departure. The Comforter				14:1-31
The vine and the branches. Abiding in love				15:1-27
Work of the Comforter in the disciples				16:1-33
The prayer of Christ for them				17:1-26
Gethsemane	26:36-46	14:32-42	22:40-46	18:1

Teachings, Parables, Miracles

A lot of cool stuff can be added right here about Jesus' teachings, parables and miracles. These are talked about in more detail in later chapters. The purpose was to prove to others who Jesus was and to prepare the disciples for bigger and better things after Jesus was gone. We can apply them to our life, too.

Jesus Predicts His Death

Matthew 20: 17-19
Mark 10: 32-34
Luke 18: 31-34

Jesus knew He was going to die. He got the gang of twelve together and gave them brief details of what was going to happen.

He told them that it would begin with a betrayal which would deliver Him into the hands of the Jewish religious leaders. They would make false accusations against Him, put Him on trial, and have Him crucified. Jesus would be an innocent man. He also knew that after He died, he would rise again on the third day.

The Betrayal and Trial of Christ				
Subject	Matthew	Mark	Luke	John
The betrayal	26:47-56	14:43-52	22:47-53	18:2-11
Christ before Annas and Caiaphas. Peter's denial	26:57, 58, 26:69-75	14:53, 54, 14:66-72	22:54-65	18:12-27
Christ before the sanhedrim	26:59-68	14:55-65	22:66-71	
Christ before Pilate	27:1, 2, 27:11-14	15:1-5	23:1-6	18:12-28
The traitor's death	27:3-10			
Christ before Herod			23:7-12	
Accusation and condemnation	27:15-26	15:6-15	23:13-25	18:29; 19:16

Judas Betrays Jesus

Matthew 26: 47-56
Mark 14: 43-52
Luke 22: 47-53
John 18: 2-11

Jesus and His disciples were at the Garden of Gethsemane. Jesus was getting all stressed out because He knew the terrible stuff that was about to happen next. He prayed while an angel was there to comfort Him.

And there appeared an angel unto him from heaven, strengthening him. And being in an agony he prayed more earnestly: and his sweat was as it were great drops of blood falling down to the ground. - Luke 22: 43, 44

Judas had already worked up a deal with the religious leaders. He would show them where Jesus was located for thirty pieces of silver. The plan was to lead them to the garden and Judas would kiss Him on the cheek so they would know which fella to arrest.

Then one of the twelve, called Judas Iscariot, went unto the chief priests, And said unto them, What will ye give me, and I will deliver him unto you? And they covenanted with him for thirty pieces of silver. And from that time he sought opportunity to betray him. - Matthew 26: 14-16

We later learn that Judas regrets ever doing this and gives them the money back. He becomes so overwhelmed with guilt for betraying Jesus that he commits suicide.

Jesus' Death

Matthew 27: 50
Mark 15: 37
Luke 23: 46
John 19: 28-30

The Crucifixion and Burial of Christ				
Subject	Matthew	Mark	Luke	John
Treatment by the soldiers	27:27-31	15:16-20	23:36,37	19:1-3
The crucifixion	27:32-38	15:21-28	23:26-34	19:17-24
The mother of Jesus at the cross				19:25-27
Mockings and railings	27:39-44	15:29-32	23:35-39	
The penitent malefactor			23:40-43	
The death of Christ	27:50	15:37	23:46	19:28-30
Darkness and other portents	27:45-53	15:33-38	23:44, 45	
The bystanders	27:54-56	15:39-41	23:47-49	
The side pierced				19:31-37
The burial	27:57-61	15:42-47	23:50-56	19:38-42
The guard of the sepulchre	27:62-66; 28:11-15			

Jesus goes through a lot of stuff before He is placed on the cross. He is beaten, mocked and spit on. He even has to carry His own cross through the town to Golgotha's hill where it reaches it's final destination.

They put nails in His hands and feet and the cross is lifted up so that everyone could see. This was how they treated criminals back in the day, but Jesus was innocent.

Jesus says seven things before He dies on the cross:

Father forgive them, for they know not what they do. - Luke 23:34
He could have been talking about the religious crowd that had Him crucified.

Or, it could be about His disciples who deserted Him and maybe Peter who denied Him three times. Maybe He was praying for us knowing how easy it is for us to forget Him in our daily lives.

Truly, I say to you, today you will be with me in paradise. - Luke 23:43
The religious leaders had mocked Him. Even now, while He is on the cross, He is being mocked by one of the thieves. However, one of them believed in who He was and asked Him to remember him when He entered His kingdom. This is how forgiving Jesus is. The kingdom is available to anyone wanting forgiveness. His love for us is full of mercy.

Woman, behold your son: behold your mother. - John 19:26-27
Even on the cross, Jesus loved His mother and was concerned for her well-being. He trusted John to be there for her. This shows His sensitive side and His concern for people. He cares.

My God, My God, why have you forsaken me? - Matthew 27:46 and Mark 15:34
At this point, Jesus was separated from God. Jesus was taking on all of the sins of the world and God, in His perfectness, had to look away. This is how it is for those that don't know Jesus as Lord and Savior. They are separated from God. This is why they feel empty.

I thirst. - John 19:28
Jesus had suffered a lot of pain. His body was drained of all the stuff that keeps it going and was shutting down. This 'living water' was now thirsty. This has a spiritual meaning because, without Jesus, we are walking through life on a hot desert looking for a watering hole. Everything we see is a mirage. Jesus is that living water that we need.

It is finished. - John 19:30
Jesus had won the victory. He lived the perfect life of obedience to God. Because of Him, we are no longer separated from Him.

Father, into your hands I commit my spirit. - Luke 23:46
Jesus was putting all of His trust in God. He knew that all that He went through was for a bigger purpose - God's perfect plan.

The Resurrection and Ascension of Christ

Subject	Matthew	Mark	Luke	John
The resurrection	28:1-10	16:1-11	24:1-12	20:1-18
Disciples going to Emmaus		16:12, 13	24:13-35	
Appearances in Jerusalem. Doubts of Thomas		16:14-18	24:36-49	20:19-29
Appearance at the sea of Tiberias				21:1-23
Appearance on the mount of Galilee	28:16-20			
Unrecorded works				20:30, 31; 21:24, 25
The ascension		16:19-20	24:50-53	

Jesus Ascends Into Heaven

Mark 16: 19-20
Luke 24: 50-53

After Jesus died on the cross, He was placed in a borrowed tomb. That means it belonged to someone else. Maybe it was like one of those grave sites that you buy while you're still living, and when you die, you can be buried there and it already be paid for. Maybe someone in the Bible days pre-ordered their tomb ahead of time and lets Jesus use it. It's a good thing that Jesus didn't buy His own tomb because He didn't need it. He rose from the dead on the third day.

When the disciples went to check on His body in the tomb, they noticed it was missing. They were freaking out and all upset. The big stone that blocked the entrance had been rolled away. Standing beside it was two men wearing shiny clothes. These weren't ordinary fellas either. They were angels and that's how they knew that Jesus had been resurrected.

For forty days (Acts 1: 3), Jesus spends a little more time with the disciples before He ascends to Heaven. He teaches them more things and shows them signs. The purpose was to strengthen them for their biggest job ever – sharing the Gospel with the world. When He felt they were ready, He joined His Father in Heaven and sits with Him at His right hand.

The Great Commission

Go ye therefore, and teach all nations, baptizing them in the name of the Father, and of the Son, and of the Holy Ghost: Teaching them to observe all things whatsoever I have commanded you: and, lo, I am with you alway, even unto the end of the world. Amen. Matthew 28: 19, 20

Before Jesus ascended into Heaven, He instructed His disciples to tell others the Good News. This is called the Great Commission and should be considered everyone's duty as a Christian (Christ follower). What do we have to do?

go
teach
baptize
make disciples

This is faith in action. That means we have to actually get up and do something. Everywhere we are is a great place to share Jesus with someone.

The Teachings of Jesus Christ

The Spiritual Harvest
John 4: 27-38

Spiritually speaking, the world is like an open field. The people that live here are part of it. Try and picture this from a farming way of thinking. You might have to put on your spiritual overalls and work boots to really get the feel of it in your mind.

Since we know that sharing Jesus with folks is our number one priority, this would be similar to planting seeds in this open field. The Great Commission would be like carrying a bag of seeds and going out into the world and spreading them out.

You might have to get more personal in some areas and help do some weeding first. This would be like helping someone on a one-on-one level. You could help them realize that they have 'weeds' growing around them and maybe work with them to get the stuff out. It's hard for seeds to take root when there's weeds smothering it and blocking the sun. Ya know?

Planting seeds is a lifelong process and many times we may never see them blossom. It could be that our job at that moment was to 'just plant seeds', while someone else comes along in that person's life and harvests. And in some cases, we may see a harvest and realize that someone else down the line had already planted the seed.

To put this in normal terms, let's say you tell someone about Jesus. A seed is planted. This person walks away and says, "Thanks for telling me about Jesus today, but my life is kinda busy right now. I don't think I have room in my schedule. Maybe later."

Five years later, this person faces a serious obstacle. Their life could be a mess and they are at rock bottom. In their mind, they remember you telling them about Jesus and all that He has done for you in your life. They make it a point to go to church that weekend. During the service, they confess their sins and accept Jesus as their Lord and Savior. That's pretty cool! And you planted that seed five years ago! Unfortunately, you didn't get to see the harvest because this person now lives 374 miles away. That's how it goes sometimes.

Salt & Light
Matthew 5: 13-16

Salt

Salt adds flavor to food and adds a little oomph. Can you imagine eating a thing of unsalted french fries from Mickey D's? It wouldn't be the same. Actually, it would be kinda boring and dull. Or how about a bag of unsalted popcorn at your local picture show? That would mean no butter either because there's salt in butter. It might taste kinda gross, wouldn't it?

As Christians, we add something to the world because we're supposed to act different. We're kinda unique. If we're living according to the Bible, we add 'flavor' because the fruits of the Spirit begin showing on the outside.

But the fruit of the Spirit is love, joy, peace, longsuffering, gentleness, goodness, faith, meekness, temperance: against such there is no law. - Galatians 5: 22, 23

Imagine walking into a room full of angry folks showing love and joy. It would add a little change of scenery and would put some positive stuff into a room of negativity. You would stand out. They might even wonder why you're so happy and junk. Some of them would want that happiness in their own life and ask you where they could get some. Of course, you would say 'Jesus'. That's why living like the world is unaffective and doesn't do God a bit of good. It makes you unuseful for His glory.

Light

As Christians, we are to be a light in the world. Jesus is that source of light within us and we should be out there letting it shine out to others. We do this in the we we act and treat people.

Here again, this involves living according to the Bible and applying what we learn. It's allowing the fruits of the Spirit to works it's way outward to other people. Think of our Christian life as someone that's holding a flashlight in a world that's full of darkness. Yes, we could just hold the flashlight for ourselves and get to where we are going in life. But, when we realize that the reason we are holding the flashlight is so that others can see, too. We might take our roles as Christians a little more seriously. We should be active out there and living a life that is pleasing to the Lord. He can use us to lead others out of darkness to Him. That's when 'being a Christian' gets pretty exciting.

Wouldn't it be cool knowing that our life could affect others in a positive way? It can if we let it. It would mean living by Jesus' example out there in the world. Be a light!

The Law
Matthew 5: 17-20

According to these verses, Jesus didn't come down here to do away with the laws that were already in place. Maybe folks thought He was some kind of weird religious sideshow that wanted to push His thoughts and ideas on people and do away with what they already had. But, according to Jesus, He didn't.

As Christians, we know that we are saved under 'grace', which means we are not bound to any laws mentioned in the Old Testament. Right? We have the New Covenant (Jesus Christ) and it replaces the Old Covenant (Moses). You with me so far?

I believe this traditional 'demon' possesses many churches today. You can find them because of its lack of fruit. Churches need to wake up! If it's not reaching others and bearing fruit, then it may want to re-evaluate itself. The church mission should be to do whatever it takes to win souls to Jesus and stand firmly on the Word of God. For a traditional church, it may involve a little modernizing. There's nothing wrong with it!

Let's get serious for a moment and look around you. Who are the lost? Do you honestly think that the way your church conducts its services would touch those people and draw them in? Or would it push them further away? Now that's something to think about.

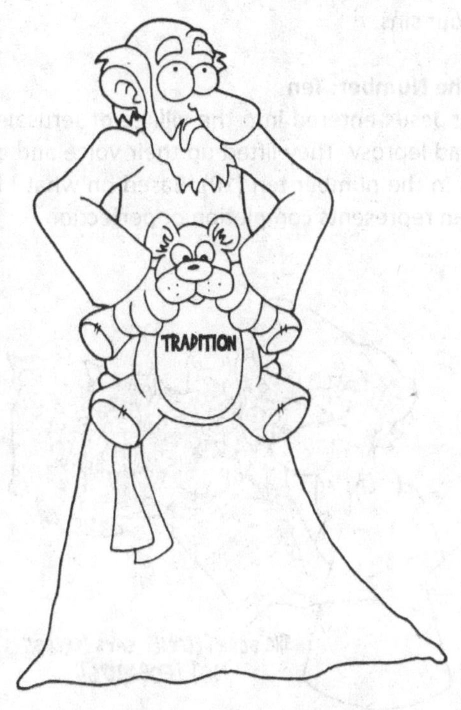

Cleansing the Ten Lepers
Luke 17: 11-19

There are a few things that stand out to me in this miracle:

The Disease: Leprosy
Having leprosy was a bad and serious thing. It was a contagious skin disease that was real nasty. According to Jewish religious practices, if you had leprosy, you were excluded from participating in their ceremonies. You would be considered ceremonially 'unclean'. You were also isolated from the community. The only way to gain acceptance again was to present yourself to the priests when your symptoms improved.

Most of the time 'sin' is symbolized in the Bible as leprosy. It destroys the body, it's contagious, and it's what separates us from God. The cure is to accept Jesus as your Lord and Savior and sincerely asking for forgiveness of your sins.

The Number: Ten

As Jesus entered into the village of Jerusalem, He encountered ten men that had leprosy. They lifted up their voice and asked Him for mercy. The key here is in the number ten (10). Based on what I have read about Biblical numbers, ten represents completion or perfection.

There are four numbers from the Bible that represent completion or perfection: 3, 7, 10, and 12. Each one is a different kind of perfection:

3 = divine perfection
7 = spiritual perfection
10 = human perfection
12 = governmental perfection
10 is the only one where humans have a part.

Let's look at the human anatomy. We have 10 fingers to do the Lord's work, 10 toes to walk upright before the Lord. God has given us, as humans, The Ten Commandments to live by for human perfection in His eyes.

The Healing

Jesus heals the ten men with leprosy and tells them to show themselves to the priests. This was to give them acceptance into the Jewish community. They were 'cleaned' but needed the priests' approval.

Being Thankful

One of the men stopped and returned to Jesus. He fell at Jesus' feet and gave Him thanks. The sad thing for this fella was that he was a Samaritan. Being a Samaritan meant that it didn't matter if he had leprosy or not, he would not be accepted by the Jews.

And what about the other nine that were cleansed? Why didn't they return to thank Jesus? Were they so eager to be accepted by the Jews and forgot to thank the Lord?

To me, I believe it's a message to Christians as well as the lost. If you are saved, Jesus has shown you mercy by forgiving you of your sins and by saving you. This mercy is also offered to everyone that doesn't know Him as Lord and Savior. The question is, "What do you do with it after you've been saved?"

The reality is that we live in a world of sin. As a Christian, we don't belong here. We're just passing through. Do we try to gain acceptance and conform to the sin that surrounds us? Or do we keep our focus on Jesus?

Just like the Samaritan, we should return to the Lord and give Him thanks by praising Him, serving Him and leading others to Him. This is how we gain human perfection in His eyes.

Curing a Devil-Possessed, Dumb and Blind Man
Matthew 12: 22-24

There was a crowd of people that day. A man from the crowd was introduced to Jesus and he had a couple of problems. He was blind and he couldn't speak. Jesus healed him. It doesn't say how Jesus did it, whether by a touch or a word. All we know is that He did and the people that were gathered were amazed. They didn't immediately follow Him as many others had done when they witnessed a miracle. They questioned Him. They just wanted to know who He was by asking, "Is not this the son of David?" They didn't recognize Him as the promised Messiah, but were more interested in his earthly position. Was He the son of David? The Pharisees gave them the answer they wanted to hear by basically telling them, "He's a worker of Satan!" There's a message here that I am battling with because it may be to me. There are things that are practiced in religions today that I don't understand. Because of my lack of understanding, I don't criticize them or say that they are wrong even though some people do. I simply choose to not focus on them. I'll explain.

I have always attended a Baptist church. That is the religion that I have been raised in - that is what I know. Some Baptist churches believe in a spiritual thing called 'shouting'. To my understanding, this is when a person becomes overjoyed with the Holy Spirit that they get an impulse to begin jumping around and start shouting. I have never experienced this in my walk with Christ. So, is this of God? I don't know. I have learned to not judge it and simply ignore it.

Some churches believe that when a person is filled with the Holy Spirit, that some begin speaking in tongues. To them, this is a spiritual language between them and God. Here again, I have never experienced this. So, is this of God? I don't know. It's not for me to decide. Even though 'speaking in tongues' is mentioned in the Bible, it's easier for me to just move on and leave it alone.

Some people claim to have a gift of prophesy. They say that the Lord gives them a word to share with others that will provide them some kind of spiritual message for their lives. This could be a message that will guide them in their walk with Christ or it could protect them from future danger. Do I have this gift? No. Do I believe this is from God? I don't know. The Bible speaks of it, but does it apply to us today? I don't

Are you seeing where I am going with this? I believe that's one of the reasons why new churches are started every day. Just because certain spiritual things aren't

Everything we do and live by must line up with the Scriptures in God's Word. God is the Father, Son, and the Holy Spirit. Jesus died on the cross for our sins and rose again. We must repent and pray for forgiveness and accept Jesus as Lord and Savior. We should also seek His righteousness by living for Him every day. This should be the basis for all religions. If not, then

124

the religion is false.

The Lord is returning one day to get His church - not churches. I feel the Lord is more concerned with our relationship with Him instead of what religion we are. We all need to be in one mind and one accord when He returns. We can't spend our valuable time judging others and their beliefs. There is so much work to be done.

Draught of Fish

Luke 5: 1-11

From a simple man's point of view, it would appear that Jesus knew where the best fishing spots were. Simon Peter was a skilled fisherman and was in the business of catching fish. This is what he knew. But, Jesus knew more. Is this a miracle story of catching fish? Or is there more?
Jesus was teaching to a crowd by the Lake of Gennesaret (Sea of Galilea). He noticed there were two empty boats parked by the bank and the fishermen that owned the boats were washing their nets. This meant these guys were finished for the day and apparently didn't catch anything.

Jesus gets in Simon Peter's boat and asks him to pull away from the shore a little so that He could continue teaching the crowd. All of a sudden, He asks Simon Peter to go out into the deeper water and to let down his net. Peter was probably wondering why Jesus would ask him to do a silly thing like this because he had already tried and didn't catch anything. But, out of obedience to Jesus, he did what He asked. The next thing you know, Simon Peter is pulling in fish. We're talking boat loads! Everyone

was so amazed that Simon Peter, James and John decided to leave their fishing stuff behind and follow Jesus.

Wait!! Weren't they already following Jesus at this point? Hmm...maybe not.

If you read Matthew 4:18-22 you'll find where Jesus called them the first time. My question is what were they doing back at their boats? Did they give up on their calling? Did they turn their backs on Jesus? I guess that's why Simon Peter called himself a sinful man in Luke 5: 8. Maybe the ministry got a little rough. Maybe they were tired of doing everything for free and decided to go back where the money was.

This would be a lesson for us that are doing ministry work for the Lord. The Lord called us for His purposes - not ours. He is leading us and wants us to be 'fishers of men'. It's true that ministry work seems a little useless at times. We get discouraged and feel like giving up. It would be a lot easier just going back to doing what we know and tend to our own business. But here's the deal. The Lord knows what He's doing. If He has called you to do something, the results of it are in His hands. It's really not up to us to decide whether our ministry is worth while or not. All we have to do is be obedient to the call.

I know for many of us, we look at the things we do in ministry. We realize we invest a lot of time on things that seem to be for 'free'. We may feel that we are missing out on money making opportunities because of this 'wasted' time that we have put into doing the Lord's work. Jesus knows this and knows how we are feeling. He wants us to put our attention on Him and not worry about anything else. If you feel you are losing out on time from making money and really look at your situation, you'll discover that He has already provided it to you in different ways.

I feel that Simon Peter, James and John were worrying about the money they were missing from following Jesus. They left their calling to go back to their business in catching fish. Unfortunately, their business didn't go so well. It took Jesus showing up and proving to them that He could provide for them in an abundance to make them realize that He had control. That one catch was probably more than they could catch in a week or possibly a month. Jesus provided.

Has the Lord given you a calling? Is He telling you to do ministry work? Are you afraid of making the step forward because of something you may have to give up? Have you given up on ministry work and decided to go back to something to make you feel more secure?

The Lord's not going 'to lead you to it without helping you through it'. He will provide the means for you to accomplish the work He has for you to do. Put Him first and He will take care of the rest. Take His advice from the last part of verse 10, "Don't be afraid; from now on you will catch men".

Let's leave our boats at the shore and follow Jesus.

Feeding The 5000
Matthew 14: 13-21

By reading the verses before this, we learn that Jesus received some bad news. His friend, John the Baptist, had died. His head was cut off and placed on a platter during King Herod's birthday party. As morbid as it sounds, this had to have been very devastating. Jesus needed some 'alone' time to be by Himself.

It's sad to know that bad things can happen to good people. For many of us, this would be a great excuse for giving up. But, Jesus didn't.

The people heard of where Jesus was and followed Him. Despite how Jesus may have felt at the time, He continued to serve the multitude. He healed their sick. This is a message to us as Christians. Yes, life will throw us curve balls. Bad things are going to happen all around us. But, we shouldn't let it get us discouraged to the point that we give up. Jesus is our example! We need to continue in our service to others and to the Lord no matter what. We must keep on keepin' on!

It tells us in verse 15 that it was getting late into the evening. I imagine the disciples were getting tired. They had probably ministered all day and were hungry and worn out. They wanted Jesus to send the people home so that they could eat. But, Jesus had a better idea!

He basically said, "Don't send them away! Let's feed them!" I can just imagine the disciples' thoughts and expressions on their faces at this point. They probably thought Jesus had lost His mind.

"Uhh, like what are we supposed to feed them? All we have are these five loaves and two fish! Get real!"

But, here again, we learn that Jesus can make things possible during impossible times. From the disciples' perception of the problem, there was no way they were going to feed all these people with the little that they had. But, as you read further, Jesus performed 'the impossible'.

There is a lesson here. We may think our problems are beyond fixing. This could be your marriage, finances, health, and the list could go on. But Jesus says in verse 18, "Bring it to me." and look at what He did. He fed them all - 5000 people? Nope, read it a little closer. It was 5000 men plus the women and children. This could have been a crowd of ten to fifteen thousand! And the crazy thing to me was that there was food left over! Impossible? Not when it comes to what my Lord can do. He can do the impossible!

Whatever you are going through today, give it to the Lord. It doesn't matter how difficult the problem may seem to you. The Lord can fix it!

Just give it to Him!

Feeding The 4000
Matthew 15: 32-39

After reading this, I realized that I had read and wrote about a miracle similar to it before in Matthew 14: 13-21. The only difference was in the number of people being fed and the amount of bread and fish they had. Why would it be important to repeat a miracle twice within two chapters of the same book? I believe it has a purpose. Let's dig into it...

Where did this miracle take place? If we look back on verse 29, we will discover that they were along the Sea of Galilee. If you do the research you'll find some interesting facts about it. I learned that the Sea of Galilee is the lowest (at sea level) freshwater lake on Earth and the water that flows to it comes from the Jordan River. Also according to a map, the Sea of Galilee sits completely surrounded by land and its water supply was for everyone around it. The travels in the ministry of Jesus seemed to go around the Sea of Galilee. Why is this important? I believe there are some symbolisms here.

Freshwater is necessary to maintain life on Earth. Without it, we would die. I believe the Sea of Galilee represents life. The Jordan River that flows to it is where Jesus got baptized. This represents the need of Jesus in our life. The fact that the Sea of Galilee is the lowest (at sea level) lake on Earth would mean that it's easily obtained. The same is true with a relationship with Jesus - it's free! All we have to do is receive it in prayer. The location of the Sea of Galilee on the map is important because it means it's for everybody. That's pretty cool!

Anyway, back to the lesson:
Why did Jesus duplicate a miracle? I believe it was to show His compassion and provision for both Jews and Gentiles. Salvation is for everyone! It was also a lesson for His followers. It taught them that if He could do a miracle once, He could do it again. I think His disciples had forgotten.

The message to us as believers is this:

Don't forget what He has done for you! We may be going through some tough times right now and it seems like there is no hope. If we were to look back on our spiritual walk with Jesus, we will see how He has helped us and how He has always made a way. We can't forget the great things He has done for us in the past. The same One that provided for us then will provide for us again.

The Lord tells us in Hebrews 13:5b, "I will never leave thee, nor forsake thee." This is a promise! Believe it! Put your trust in the Lord! The miracle in your life is on its way!

Healing a Lame Man in Bethesda
John 5: 1-16

Here we have a story of a man with a problem. He is paralyzed and, according to the scriptures, he had been that way for thirty eight years. The sad thing is that he didn't know who Jesus was. He had been coming to this pool called Bethesda with the hopes of getting in and being healed. The Bible says that an angel would come down at certain times and stir the water causing the first one to enter to be healed of whatever disease they had. This guy's problem was that he could never get in fast enough. People were always getting in front of him. That's when Jesus showed up and with a word the man was healed.

The story ends with the Jews getting upset because Jesus had worked on a Sabbath day. This is a great miracle! It shows Jesus' compassion for people even though they don't call out to Him. It shows His power as the Great Physician. It tells us that Jesus offers hope when all hope is gone. And I'm sure there are more things this miracle illustrates.

A few things stood out to me as I read this and 'hit' me as a little strange:

1. Bethesda was a pool inside of the gates in Jerusalem. It had miracle working powers. When an angel would stir the water, people could be healed. To me, it sounds odd because throughout the Bible, God gets the glory for miracles and healing - not angels. This miracle pool powered by angels puts the focus on them. Was this and could this have been some sort of pagan place where people worshiped idols? If so, this man and all of the other sick people were seeking a miracle at the wrong place.

2. What was the point of mentioning that Bethesda had 'five porches'? Is there significance in that? It just doesn't fit in. Unless, it symbolized something else.

3. Why did the scripture have to tell how long the man had suffered with his infirmity? Did we need to know that he suffered 38 years? Or do these numbers have a deeper meaning? And what was his sin that caused his suffering?

4. Why did Jesus ask the man, "Do you want to be made well?" Wouldn't you think that a man who had suffered for 38 years would want to be better? It was almost a strange question to ask.

What if one of the purposes behind this miracle was to be a message to the Jews and the nation of Israel? The lame man would represent Israel as a nation that sinned against God by disobeying him. It had became paralyzed by it's sin and it's teaching of Judaism.

The five porches could represent the five books used by the Jews that make up the Torah. The Torah, Five Books of Moses, is what legally makes up the Judaism religion.

Thirty eight years is also mentioned in Deuteronomy 2:14. Israel's 38 years of wandering in the wilderness after the Law was given had proved that Israel was helpless without their Messiah. But even after the Messiah came to His people and offered them healing, their response was similar to that of this lame man. As the lame man still thought that his healing must come through the waters of the pool, so the Jewish people continued to believe that somehow their salvation was tied up with trying to keep the Law, as taught by the teachings of Judaism.

By asking, "Do you want to be made well?" Jesus is offering a solution to Israel's problem if they wanted it. Follow Him. It's the relationship with Jesus and not the religion that will save you. I may be out in 'left field' with this one, but it really makes sense if you think about it.

Healing a Man's Withered Hand
Matthew 12: 9-14

There are some cool things about this miracle that really stood out to me. The irony of it is that this man needed a 'helping hand' - literally. But, there was a problem. There were rules to follow. You couldn't help someone on a Sabbath day unless it was life threatening. These Pharisees were serious about it. It was the rule!

That's the great thing about my Lord and Savior. Jesus doesn't follow man-made rules! There are no restrictions - no limitations! This scripture can apply to almost anything we do to serve the Lord and in our efforts in helping others.

One of the best ways we can help others is through sharing the Word of God. There should be no limit as to how we do it as long as we align it with the Bible as a whole. This message could be to churches all over the world that hold tight to its traditions - its rules. We can't limit God!

In our praise and worship, are we limited to a specific style? If we are to reach the world in ministry, we have to be open-minded to the Spirit's leading. This could offend a lot of people in their traditions, but who are we following here, man or God?

This could be a message to someone out there that refuses to associate themselves with a particular person in need because of their religious preference or their individual sin. It's like we are afraid to reach out to someone and help them because of the rules we have set and made for ourselves.

It would be like not helping a person struggling with a drug addiction because we are afraid of being seen around them. We have become overtaken by the fear of being noticed by our fellow Christian brothers and sisters and worrying about what they may think about us. Maybe a person with different religious beliefs needed help and we turned them away because they weren't the same as we are. What it boils down to is this...does it really matter? They need help!

I feel this message is about making our own rules when it comes to helping someone out there. People are people regardless of race, religion and any other classification we put on them. Jesus wasn't all about rules when it came to the love He had for folks. He loves us all!

We are to show His example by helping everyone regardless of who they are or what we think of them. If they come into our path needing a 'helping hand', we should offer it to them with no restrictions. By doing this, they will see Jesus working in us and through us. We can't be held down by rules. Jesus wasn't!

Allow the Holy Spirit to talk to you today and really listen. Jesus didn't allow rules to hold Him back from His work and neither should you. What man-made traditions or rules are you holding onto? Don't let them hinder you from doing the work God has called YOU to do.

Be a 'helping hand' to someone for the Lord - with no limitations!

Healing the Bowed Woman
Luke 13: 10-17

When I first read this, I kept thinking about the woman with the disease. What was wrong with her? What could possibly cause her to be bowed like this? The scripture tells me that she had a 'spirit of infirmity'. This means there was a spiritual problem going on. And then this miracle ends with a debate on whether to work on a Sabbath day. This is some confusing stuff! What's it all about? Let's take it slow...

Jesus Was Teaching In a Synagogue on Sabbath
The miracle begins as Jesus is teaching in the synagogue. I'm sure it was a normal Sabbath day as the people gathered together as they heard the message, except this time the speaker was Jesus.

There Was a Woman with a Spirit of Infirmity
In the congregation that day was a lady sitting there, hearing the message, as she has done for years on the Sabbath. This lady had something wrong with her. She was bowed over. Because it says she had a spirit of infirmity tells me that she had some spiritual issues going on. It also says that she had been suffering with it for 18 years. That's a long time! Don'tcha think? It would be easy to say that despite her illness, she continued to attend the services at the

synagogue. She didn't let it stop her. It's easy to let things get you down to stop serving or to let them prevent you from going to church. But, I think in this case, she may have been attending for the wrong reason or that she wasn't growing spiritually. This would be similar to a plant that doesn't get water and sunlight. It will begin bowing over before it eventually dies. Being 'bowed over' could represent her spiritual deterioration. She wasn't getting fed spiritually.

This Woman Was a Daughter of Abraham

The scripture mentions that this woman was a descendant of Abraham. To include this in the passage tells me that this was a 'blood line' problem. This deterioration problem could have begun with her generations before her.

Another point that stands out is that the woman did not come to Jesus to receive her miracle. He came to her. She may have been content with her problem. Jesus healed her anyway.

Working on the Sabbath

After the woman was healed, the ruler of the synagogue spoke up. Instead of thanking Jesus for what he done for the woman, he was more focused on the 'broken' law of working on the Sabbath. This tells me that he was more concerned with the laws than he was for the people that attended. Jesus corrected him and his adversaries were ashamed.

Here's the deal:

Jesus is a 'people' person. All that He has done and is going to do is for us. He died on the cross so that we could live. All we have to do is accept Him as our Lord and Savior. He is concerned with our spiritual well-being and wants a strong relationship with us. The Bible is full of 'one on one' miracles and relationships between someone

and Jesus.

Many churches today are more concerned with their rules and regulations, their programs, and their ritualistic stuff. Because of their focus, the people that attend their services are suffering spiritually. Yes, they may 'show up' for church but they are not getting fed. Church is a place for worship and for learning about Jesus Christ: the cross, the blood, sin, etc. A church that does not center around or does not stand on the foundation of Jesus, the people will suffer.

It is time for the church to go back to the fundamentals of what Jesus was teaching. We need to focus on Him in our worship. If we don't, then church will be more of a social club and the body will begin to deteriorate – bowing over with a spiritual infirmity.

How is your walk with Jesus today? Are you 'on fire' spiritually? If not, it could be caused from lack of spiritual nutrition. Check your food source - it could be contaminated.

Healing the Deaf and Dumb Man
Mark 7: 31-37

Here we have a man with some problems. He couldn't hear and he had a speech impediment. Poor guy!! It doesn't say that he couldn't speak, but that he couldn't speak properly. Either way, it was a problem and needed a touch from Jesus. Jesus pulled him aside and touched his ears and tongue and SHAZAM!!...he was healed! Awesome miracle! The end? I believe there is more to this...
Jesus entered into the coasts of Decapolis. A crowd brings a man to Him and asks Him to please heal him of his deaf and speech problem. Jesus could have healed him right then and there without a touch or a word. He could've said, "Your faith has made you whole" and everything would have worked out fine, but He didn't. There was a hindrance in this man in receiving his miracle. What was it?

These verses tell us that this man was in a crowd and Jesus had to pull him aside before He performed the miracle. Part of a crowd? Hmm...

There are two paths we can follow in life: the path of the world and the path to Jesus. This man had followed the path to Jesus. That's good! However, for this man, he didn't follow this path on his own. He came as part of a crowd.

This brings up a couple of questions. Why didn't the man ask Jesus personally for his miracle? Was he truly looking for Jesus or was he just following his friends?

In my mind, this is similar to people that go to church. What is their purpose for going? Are they seeking a personal relationship with Jesus and desiring to grow as a Christian or is it just to be part of the church crowd? Does a person think that they become saved by 'just going to church'? It's great to have Christian friends and being able to fellowship with them is awesome, but if it's the only reason we go to church, then it becomes more of a social club. And just going to church doesn't save us. You know that, right?

Because the man was deaf and couldn't speak properly could be a symbolism for the fact that he was influenced by the crowd. He didn't have his own 'identity' because he came and went with the crowd. He had 'no voice' and didn't 'hear' when it came to spiritual matters because he was more concerned with what the crowd was doing.

When Jesus performed the miracle for the man, He gave him something personal. He pulled him from the crowd into a personal one-on-one relationship. Then, He gave him a personal touch, both to his tongue and to his ears. Now the man had his own identity and oneness with his Savior.
There is a lesson here for us, too.

Do you have a personal relationship with Jesus? Or is your relationship more with the people of the church and its activities? Jesus is calling you from the crowd and wants you to experience a relationship with Him 'one-on-one' as an individual. If you are not saved, ask Jesus to come into your life today. If going to church has become a social club for you, put your focus back on the Lord. This is what it's all about. It's about Him!

Let's step out and experience a 'one-on-one' relationship with Jesus Christ.

Healing The Epileptic Boy
Mark 9: 14-29

After reading this I realize that Jesus walked into a deep religious discussion. It appears to me that someone brought forth a problem. This person's son had a dumb spirit - he had epilepsy. There were two groups there to help with the situation; the disciples, who were followers and believers in Jesus, and the scribes, who were teachers of the law. The problem was that neither of them could help.

I imagine the disciples tried everything they could in their strength to minister to the boy. At the same time, the scribes probably pulled out their rule books and gave the boy direction from their laws and regulations. According to the scripture, none of it helped. Fortunately, Jesus showed up.

Jesus requested the boy to be brought to Him and sees the problem. He meets the father of the boy and discovers that this problem has been going on for awhile. Jesus also questions the father's belief in Him. There appears to be some doubt. Uh oh!

Jesus performed the miracle, but told His disciples that it was only through prayer and fasting that they could see it

happen in their lives.

There's a lot of stuff going on in these verses. I think this whole miracle is about a lesson of faith. What is faith? Faith is believing and trusting in Jesus alone. That's where a personal relationship with Jesus is crucial.

The disciples may have put their faith in their own works. The scribes may have put their faith in their laws and religion. The boy's father may have put his faith in man. But when it came down to receiving the miracle, it was about having faith in Jesus. Prayer and fasting is how we surrender to the fact that Jesus is Lord of our lives and that only He can provide our miracle.

What is the message here for us? Here it is:

We are also a faithless generation and everybody wants a miracle in their life. We can run to the Christians for help. We could run to the religious leaders. But, the One we really need to run to is Jesus Christ! We need to surrender our problems to Him with a one-on-one personal relationship and believe that only He can provide the miracle.

The first step is giving your life to Him. Ask Him to come into your life and save you! If you continue to run in the other directions, you'll never receive your miracle. Go straight to the source. If you're a Christian today, put your faith in Jesus Christ alone. Don't put your faith in others or yourself and not in your religion. It won't work! It's about your relationship with Jesus and believing and trusting only in Him.

Healing The Gentile Woman's Daughter
Matthew 15: 21-28

At first this sounded to me like Jesus and His disciples didn't want to help this woman's daughter. This woman was crying out to Jesus for help and He was silent. The disciples wanted to send her away. Now this doesn't sound like the Jesus I know. I have always been taught that He loves everyone and wouldn't turn someone away. He did, however, heal the girl in the end and she was made whole, but what was the purpose of this miracle? This could be interesting.

Starting at the beginning, Jesus and His disciples went to the coasts of Tyre and Sidon. These were powerful states in the land of Canaan (or Phoenicia). They were among the greatest sea traders at the time and were famous for producing a purple dye that they used in the textiles that they traded. Textiles is another word for stuff like fabric, cloth...ya know the stuff our clothes are made of. I had to look it up. Another interesting fact about the Canaanites is that they worshiped several gods with the main one being named Baal. This made the Canaanites pagans.

This woman from Canaan cries out to Jesus, "Have mercy on me!" This tells me that her pagan god wasn't working out for her and that she needed Jesus right away. It was almost like she was turning away from her pagan religion or cult to find something that works - a faith in Jesus Christ!

I think Jesus hesitated for a few reasons. He wanted to see the disciples' reaction and how they would respond to a pagan woman in need. Keep in mind; people from Canaan were despised for their religion and their religious practices. Next, He wanted to see the woman's reaction by refusing to help her. Would she turn to another god for help, bouncing from religion to religion until she found a solution she liked? But the woman persisted and her faith in Jesus resulted in the miracle.

The message here to me is this:

There are people in the world today that worship other gods. I'm not talking about the things people treat as gods like money and material things. I'm talking about actual religions where God, Jesus, and the Holy Spirit are not involved. Can you believe that? We, as Christians, shouldn't push them away. We can't just witness to 'unsaved' people that don't know Jesus on a personal level. We need to witness to the ones that don't know Him at all - the pagans.

We may fear that they will try and persuade us to their religion, but we have nothing to fear. Their gods are a lie and we need to share with them the Truth! You hearing me? We can't just sit back and wait for their gods to fail them. We need to talk with them about Jesus when the opportunity comes around.

Here's an interesting fact:

There are festivals held every year in places all over the world. It's called Pagan Pride Day and it started back in the early 1990's. A ribbon is worn as a symbol of being proud to be a pagan. Ironically, the color of this ribbon is purple - the color used by the Canaanites. Isn't that cool?

Healing The Man Born Blind
John 9: 1-7

Here we have a blind man that had been this way since he was born. This was a problem that he and his parents had been dealing with until this day that Jesus passed by. It was thought in those days, that if a person had a disability, it was created by sin. It was either a sin from the disabled person or from their parents. Say what?

The disciples questioned Jesus about this man and wanted to know, "Who sinned?" His answer was that his disability wasn't created by the sin of neither the man nor his parents, but so that the works of God should be manifested

in him.

I know that any time a person is mentioned being blind, it references to a person's spiritual blindness; being blind to the truth of knowing Jesus Christ. I know from reading the entire chapter that the blind man's parents were spiritually blind because they were more interested in their status in the synagogue. Also, the Pharisees were spiritually blind because they were more concerned with following the 'rule book' of Moses instead of the One that gave the rules to begin with. They were all confronted with it after Jesus heals the man and his sight was restored. It's an awesome miracle! But, was there more?

Verse 3 sticks in my head the most and after reading it, I can't help but picture kids born in the world today with disabilities and wonder why they have to be this way. Is it bad genetics or was it caused by sinful acts created by their parents? Or could it be possible that God allowed them to be this way for a reason?

There are many parents out there today that probably wonder why their kids are sick or why they died. I'm sure many of them question God or even question themselves and wonder, "Where did I go wrong?" or "What did I do?" Maybe the answer has nothing to do with us.

I have seen and talked with parents that have given up on God and Christianity because their child dies or has a disability. They blame it on God because they feel that He allowed this to happen to them or took their child away. This is a sad situation and it's hard to explain why this happens. Most of the time we can't give a good explanation or we can just simply say 'it was God's will'. This doesn't answer their question. It becomes a touchy subject - a spiritual one.

If a woman who is a drug addict becomes pregnant, the chances of having a child with a birth defect are increased. Her sin could manifest itself in that child. The same is true in an alcoholic or any other sinful act. That I can understand, but what about parents who are Christians and live right? What about them?

Here's my thinking. This world is not our home. Do you agree? It is a temporary place and if you're saved, you are just passing by. We are here until Jesus returns. So, what are we to do while we are here? The Bible says to seek His righteousness and to become more like Jesus. We are also to become disciples (followers of Jesus) with a purpose of leading others to Him. As

Christians, the Lord uses us for His glory. This means everything! Not only does He use us, but He uses our abilities, our home, our money, and even our children.

You are probably thinking, "Now, I understood it all until the last part. How can God get glory by using my child, especially one with a birth defect? Why would a merciful God create a child and allow it to suffer or die? Where's the glory in that?"

Based on reading John 9: 8-41, this blind man was healed and he went to his neighbors, family, and the Pharisees. Everyone saw this new 'transformation' and everyone's life was touched. God worked through this disabled man to reach others and His message was delivered. All of these people knew this blind man and somehow were associated with his life. Many of them blamed his parents for him being this way. Some of them may have felt sorry for him, but the fact is that they knew him and his life. Now they knew that Jesus was part of it.

All of us at one time were spiritually blind. For many of us, it took a drastic event to open our eyes and see Jesus. We would always ignore the Christian that would invite us to church and their attempts to witness to us. It was that devastating calamity that brought us to our knees. It's sad, but we live in a world with people with hardened hearts. The Lord has to wake us up and sometimes it may take doing it through our kids.

I believe all children are gifts from God, but they belong to Him. The same God, that sent His Son to suffer and die for us to get our attention, will use our children, too. I feel that children with disabilities are God's special tools to reach others. It may not be to reach us as parents, but it could be to reach the ones he or she will encounter as they grow up. One thing is for certain, with every disabled child or death of a child, a spiritual conflict arises among the ones that know them. Their eyes are spiritually opened, they are focused on God, and they are left with the question of whether to believe or not. We could either say that God is mean and choose to be bitter and hate Him or we could recognize that God loves the world and chose the child to be used to reach others for His glory.

I can imagine that having a child with a disability or having a child to die would be devastating. But, seeing how their life touches the lives of others and how it brings God into the equation is amazing. It's very much like the same scenario as the birth of Jesus. It was through this child, His pain, suffering and death, that a world could be saved.

There's something humbling about talking with a child or person with a disability. You realize how blessed you are and how you shouldn't take the simple things in life for granted. And when this disabled person goes around talking about Jesus and their love for Him, it wakes you up!

I had the chance to speak with a blind man one time. The guy couldn't see, but yet he read his Bible. How is that possible? They make Bibles for the blind. It's basically a book with what I call 'bumpy dots' in them so that the disabled person could use their fingers to feel around the page and read. It's pretty cool.

Here's the eye opener for me. If this man is putting aside his disability of being able to see to read God's Word, why is it so hard for a person with good vision to do it. Seeing him read his Bible convicted my heart and made me want to read mine more. You see where I'm going with this?

I have seen a man in a wheel chair preaching before. He could have easily just said, "Nope. Ain't doing it. I'm disabled!" But no, he was up there spreading God's Word. If he could do it with a disability, then what's my excuse?

Man, that's enough to get you on fire! I guess the message is that God uses disabled people to wake the world up and it works! He has a purpose behind everything! God is God! You know what I'm saying?

Healing the Man with Dropsy
Luke 14: 1-6

Jesus was eating bread on the Sabbath with the chief Pharisees. The Pharisees were the

religious leaders of the Jewish religion during those days. They had their rules and regulations and despised what Jesus was 'bringing to the table', yet they invited Him over to 'eat' anyway. This was like a trap! I believe they wanted to find a reason to charge Him with something. He was being watched. Jesus noticed a man that was there. This man had a disease called 'dropsy'.

Let's talk about this disease for a moment because I believe this is the main point of the message.

Dropsy? What is it? I have never heard of this disease before so I looked it up on the Internet. Here's what it tells me. Dropsy is an old word used to describe an abnormal accumulation of fluid beneath the skin, or in one or more cavities of the body. To put this in a spiritual sense, this man had a 'build up' of body fluid (natural water) instead of the 'living water' that Jesus freely offers. Pretty cool, huh?

We know from the Bible that Jesus is the source for 'living water'. John 7: 38 tells us, *"He that believeth on me, as the scripture hath said, out of his belly shall flow rivers of living water."* This man from the scripture in Luke 14 was running on the wrong kind of water and Jesus knew it. Before Jesus healed the man, he asked a question to Jewish leaders "Is it lawful to heal on the Sabbath day?" The Pharisees and the lawyers did not answer. Why? This would have been a great opportunity for them to confront Jesus with their beliefs, but instead they 'held their peace'. It was like they wanted to know more. At the moment, they could have realized their way of believing didn't make sense. They may have been confronted with their own religious practices and were forced to think about them. They were speechless!

The man didn't come to Jesus for the miracle. Jesus came to him. This tells me the man

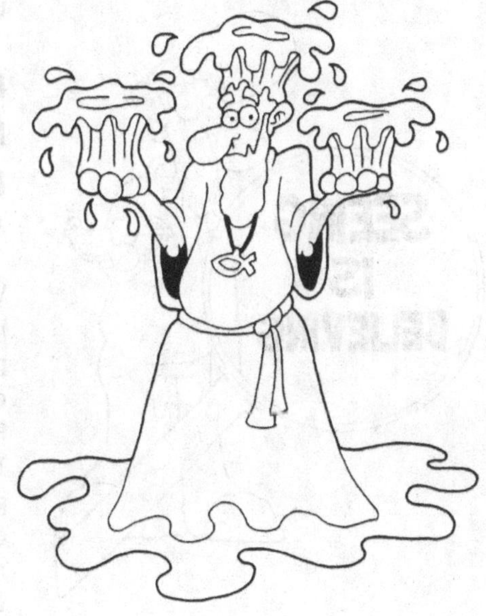

didn't know he had a problem or maybe he was content with it. It could be that the man didn't know where to go for his miracle. Jesus shows him and heals the man and sends him on his way!

Here again is another example to the body of Christ. We, as Christians, should be filled with 'living water'. John 7:38 tells us that we 'shall flow rivers of living water'. A river that flows is moving and it flows to others. It's ALIVE!! It doesn't lie stagnant or build up. Water that sits begins to stink. Jesus doesn't give stagnant water! He gives LIVING water!

Take a look at your life. Are you spiritually flowing with the water that Jesus offers? If so, you should be alive and active. You should have joy, happiness, and be doing something! A life without living water is a life that's dead. There's no joy! It doesn't produce fruit because it doesn't influence people and doesn't lead them to Jesus.

Who wants to live like a septic tank anyway? This kind of life stinks!

What kind of water do you have today? Is it 'living' or is 'just building up'? If you're not alive, ask Jesus for a miracle. Ask Him for the 'living water' that He freely gives. Let Him fill you with life, so that through you others can be reached and will know Jesus as their Lord and Savior.

Healing The Nobleman's Son of Fever
John 4: 46-54

We live in a world where 'seeing is believing'. This is why many people don't want to be saved or experience what God has to offer. First, they don't believe in God. They don't see Him and all the great miraculous things He has done.

We, as Christians, try to witness to these people, but they choose not to believe because they are unable to see. They are blind as a bat! We may try and enter into a debate with them by sharing what we have seen, but their eyes are blind because they want to 'see' before they 'believe'. You with me? This is what this scripture is talking about.

Here we have a man that has walked 20 miles to meet Jesus. His son is about to die. Jesus is his last resort. He may have put his faith in the physicians. He may have tried to reach out to his friends. He was hanging on by a string, but he remembered a man named Jesus. I'm glad he had a good memory!

As the scripture begins, Jesus enters Cana in Galilee. A royal official comes to Him and begs Him to come and heal his son because he was about to die. Being a royal official tells me the man had power. He even had servants. He was probably very wealthy. For him to put that power aside to meet Jesus tells me he had faith. He also called Him 'Sir'. To me, this was his way of showing respect as he humbled himself in the presence of the Lord.

Jesus must have known that this man and the people of the town had a problem with belief. They may have wanted to see a miracle first. For a second, the man may have questioned his own motives for coming to Jesus. Was it because He was his last resort when everything else didn't work? Or did he really believe that Jesus could do the impossible? The man chose to believe.

At that moment Jesus didn't 'show' him a miracle. The man didn't 'see' the miracle before his eyes. Jesus only 'spoke' it into existence. This man had to act upon his belief. He had to walk back home believing that Jesus had healed his son. I bet this was hard for him to do. Anybody else would have asked Jesus to come to their house and perform the miracle so that they could see it happen. This was truly an act of faith. This miracle ends with the boy receiving his health. His life was restored. It was by belief, faith,

and the power of Jesus and His Word that made him whole.

There's a message to us today in this. Are you waiting for a sign before you start believing in Jesus? Are you waiting for things to change in your life without believing that Jesus can do it?

The miracle in your life begins with you! That's right! Believe that He can and wants to do it! Act on that belief in faith with the attitude that it has already been done! Then, you will see it come to pass!

Are you saved today? If not, why not? Is it because you don't believe in God? Are you waiting to 'see' that miraculous sign before you start believing? Take a look at the Christians whose lives have been changed. Look at the world around you. It could be that you have already 'seen'.

Now it's your turn to believe.

Healing the Sick at Evening
Matthew 8: 16-17

Jesus had a busy day and it wasn't over. He had already performed miracles during the day and when the evening came, many that were possessed with devils were brought to Him. Evening around my home is around six o'clock. When I get home from working, I want to relax. I want to kick back on the sofa, click the television on and think about something else other than work. Aren't you the same way?

Jesus had a loving and serving spirit as mentioned in this verse. People could bring someone to Him and He would focus on their needs. The same is true for us today! The Lord knows we have or will have problems. He wants us to bring those problems to Him in prayer. He has the remedy! There's healing power in the words of Jesus. Let's go get some!

I couldn't help but notice from this verse that the people that came to Him were 'devil possessed'. The first thought that crossed my mind was a scene from Hollywood from the movie 'Exorcist'. You know the movie - young girl, devil possession, her head would spin a full 360 degree circle, and the famous green vomit that would shoot from her mouth. OK! Now you remember! I honestly don't think these people were like that and I don't think Hollywood's version of devil possession is possible. There are some that may disagree and everyone is entitled to their own opinion. Anyway...

Let's think about something for a moment. For a person to be devil possessed, a devil would have to live inside that person. The only power that Satan and his devils have is through temptations and lies. By falling into the traps of temptation and lies, it will turn into sin and when sin has manifested itself in us, we basically become under the control of the devil and Satan himself. I believe this is devil possession. Does that make sense?

A man tries drugs for the first time and then becomes addicted. The drugs begin controlling his life. I believe he would be considered devil possessed. Only by surrendering his life to Jesus will he be released. Without Him, he will be destroyed by death of his own design. Plus, he has affected and hurt the lives of those around him.

Another important thing about this verse is that a prophecy was fulfilled. It refers to Isaiah 53:4-5:

Surely he hath borne our griefs, and carried our sorrows: yet we did esteem him stricken, smitten of God, and afflicted. But he was wounded for our transgressions, he was bruised for our iniquities: the chastisement of our peace was upon him; and with his stripes we are healed.

It was prophesied in the Old Testament that a simple servant would come; our Promised Messiah. Even though He was unattractive and the world despised Him, He would take away our pain and sufferings. It would take someone very powerful to be able to do this.

The world still despises and rejects Him today. They don't know how real His power is. Let me tell you from experience, He can change you and make life better. Do you want a change in your life? Ask the Lord to come into your life and save you.

Healing Two Blind Men
Matthew 9: 27-31

Something happened to me as a kid about twenty five years ago that changed my entire life. I will always remember that day. One of my friends from school and I had been discussing the Bible, Jesus, and the whole religion thing. I remember having several questions and concerns about my own spiritual being. You know? It was like my eyes became opened to see a terrible truth. I was lost and needed a Savior. I knew at that moment I needed Jesus Christ in my life!

I wasn't at a church, or at a Revival Camp Meeting, or even at a church youth function. I was at home! What was I going to do about it? I didn't know what praying was and I sure didn't know how to take the steps of receiving Christ into my life. I remember asking my mother how to be saved. She told me and I took off to the quietest place in the house - the bathroom! I may be the only person in this world that has gotten saved in a bathroom, but it will be a day I will always remember. It was the day I received my sight!

According to the scripture, two blind men needed something. They wanted mercy and they believed that Jesus could give it to them. Jesus knew what they really needed - new sight. And He gladly gave it.

There are so many people walking around this world in the dark. They are blind to the truth about Jesus and His saving power. They don't realize it because they are hanging around people that are just as blind as they are.

I may be talking to you today. If you don't know Jesus as your Lord and Savior, you are lost. If you can't remember a time when you prayed for Jesus to come into your life and save you, you are lost. You are lost!! But, there's hope and you have a choice to make.

Do you want to be saved? Do you? If so, continue reading…

Step 1

The first step is to recognize that you are lost. I believe you have already done that today. Right?

Step 2

The second step is to repent. Repent? What is that? It's praying and asking the Lord to forgive you of all of your sins. You know – the rotten stuff!

Step 3

The last step is to receive. Ask Him to come into your life. Ask Him to save you and He will!

Romans 10:13 tells us, *"For whosoever shall call upon the name of the Lord shall be saved."* It's very simple! If you accepted Jesus Christ today, you made a wise choice.

Healing the Hemorrhaging Woman
Matthew 9: 20-22

I want to believe that this is a story of a woman's strong faith and the great power of Jesus. At first, it sounds like she had so much faith that all she had to do was touch His garment to be healed. But, as I look deeper into this, I don't think that's the case.

Here we have a woman with a big problem in her life. She had been suffering with it for twelve years. 12 years!! That's a long time to carry a burden day in and day out. I'm sure she knew who Jesus was and I'm sure she knew He could heal her. I imagine she knew this stuff twelve years ago, too. My question is, "Why didn't she come to Jesus 'personally' back when the problem first began?"

In the Bible, people needing a miracle would come to Jesus 'face-to-face'. This woman didn't. It was almost like she secretly wanted the miracle without the confrontation. Are you seeing what I'm seeing? It's almost like wanting the blessings that the Lord gives without having the personal relationship first.

In my mind, I picture people today that want miracles in their life, but yet they are not willing to serve the Lord. They want people to pray for them and their problems, but they are not willing to live their life according to the way the Bible tells them. Instead of seeking Him personally, they want Bible tracts and prayer cloths.

Let me tell you something. Jesus wants a relationship! Matthew 6:33 tells us:

"But seek ye first the kingdom of God, and his righteousness; and all these things shall be added unto you."

This is a message to us that we really need to hear. If we are to have our prayers answered, we need to first KNOW the One that can answer and then be more like Him by seeking His righteousness. I don't believe this woman was healed when she touched His garment. I think it was when He turned to her and she saw Him 'face-to-face' that she got her miracle.

Do you want miracles in your life? Seek Jesus 'face-to-face' and start living your life for Him.

Devils Entering a Herd of Swine

Mark 5: 1-20

It may sound like a simple exorcism where a man (or two as mentioned in Matthew 8: 28-34) was devil possessed. He became healed by the words of Jesus. But, when you compare it to the Scriptures in Matthew and Luke, there are some different details mentioned. I do not know why there are different accounts, but the main message is the same.

The Scripture tells us that Jesus was in the country of the Gadarenes. This was the country of Gadara (tribe of Gad). When you read Numbers (Chapter 32), you'll discover that these Gadarenes had some unfinished work to do for the Lord. They were to combine forces with other tribes to possess the land God had promised. The Gadarenes chose to sit still. The Lord was angry with them, but they were content to stay where they were. Sin starts with being content with our walk and not obeying God. That's called DISOBEDIENCE!

These Gads were originally in the cattle and sheep business but chose a different occupation. They put aside their beliefs and pursued a career in raising pigs. Based on Jewish customs, it was considered 'unclean' to eat pork but yet this country raised pigs. It says there were 2000 of them. That tells me that they weren't ordinary pets like they are here in the South, but possibly their way of producing an income.

Sin had gradually become part of this country's way of life. They rebelled against God and compromised their faith. The man possessed with the devils lived in the tombs! Sounds creepy! Here again is another example of an 'unclean' act according to Jewish customs, but it symbolizes how great sin had become. This man was a product of the sin of the country! He was the first person Jesus saw when He arrived at the shores of Gadara.

This man was possessed with devils and no man could bind him down or tame him. Chains didn't work either! These devils had a name, Legion, because there were so many! Sin at its fullest was represented in this man, but he knew who Jesus was and worshiped Him. He knew the power of the Lord.

The devils begged Jesus to not remove them from the country but to send them into the swine. Jesus could have destroyed them right then and there on the spot, but there was more to learn from this miracle. He sent the devils to the swine. Then the swine jumped a cliff and choked (died). The caretakers of the swine ran back and told others of what had happened. When they had seen what Jesus had done, instead of praising Him for healing the possessed man, they told Him to leave because of the damage he had caused to their swine, their money maker.

I believe this message is for America. Our country was built on the foundation of Jesus Christ. Our focus was on Him, but we have allowed sin to corrupt our existence and purpose for being here. We have compromised our original beliefs in Him to accommodate sin in our lives. Take a look at our country today. Look at the mess we've made. We have exchanged our God for the love of money and sin. Now we're watching it as it falls off the cliff. Our money makers are being destroyed.

There is hope! Jesus is standing at the shoreline ready to heal us. All we need to do is run to Him and worship Him. Don't tell Him to leave! Let's join together and realize that we need Him in our country. Let's start over and remember our motto, 'In God We Trust'!

The Scripture ends with the healed man wanting to go with Jesus, but Jesus told him to go home and tell his friends of the great things the Lord had done. And he did.
I, too, am a product of the sin in America, but I choose to live for the Lord. I am telling you, America, of how great the Lord is. Turn to Him! America, it's your choice.

Jesus Calms the Storm
Matthew 8: 23-27

I love this miracle. There is so much to learn in these few verses and everyone can apply it to their own individual lives. This wasn't an ordinary boat ride! Oh, no! These guys weren't taking a break from ministry work and

enjoying a nice relaxing vacation on the lake. Even though that would've been great, there was definitely more to this adventure!

It's a simple message, too. The boat represents our life. It's the life of both Christians and non-Christians. We're all on the open sea! The difference in our boats is whether Jesus is on it or not! I'm glad He's on mine! Aren't you?

One thing we can guarantee - storms are coming! We could be sailing smoothly right now, but the storms will come. We just don't know when.

What are the storms of life? I could put it simply by saying, "Anything that stresses me out!" This could be anything from a small argument with your spouse to severe financial problems. Believe me, you'll recognize the storm when it hits.

According to Verse 24, the storm was a bad one. The waves were coming into the boat! There was a potential chance of the boat actually sinking. I bet it was scary! Where was Jesus at? Didn't He know there was a storm happening? If so, why did He allow it to happen? The verse said He was asleep! Was He just going to lay there while the waves crashed down on the boat until it sank? Did He care? These are the same questions we ask when we are in the midst of a storm. I believe there's a lesson here.

The disciples had a couple of choices. They could have tried to do something in their own strength. This may or may not have worked. Or they could have totally relied on Jesus to fix the problem. I believe the Lord allows us to struggle with the storm to show us how weak we really are. I call this process - a Pride Buster. We have to push aside pride and seek the Lord. In verse 25, it says they woke Him up and asked for His help. The Lord moves for us in the same way through prayer. If you're in a storm, the best thing you can do is pray and give it to the Lord.

Can you see these disciples running around in a panic? They were scared to death! In their minds, I'm sure they were thinking, "What am I going to do now?" Jesus knew they had little faith. It's easy to say we have faith in the good times. How do we react when our faith is put to the test in the bad times? Jesus calmed the storm and the disciples were amazed. Their faith in Jesus became stronger.

You're on a boat today on life's sea. It may be smooth sailing but a storm is on its way. Do you have enough faith in Jesus to believe He can calm the sea? You may be in a storm today. Wake Jesus up by praying. Give Him full control of the storm you're in.

But most importantly, invite Jesus into your boat. If you don't know Him as Lord and Savior, do it today!

Jesus Heals a Blind Man
Luke 18: 35-43

Right Place At The Right Time?

A few thoughts crossed my mind about this situation. First, what was a blind man doing on the side of the road? Secondly, what are the chances of him being there when Jesus and the crowd of followers passed by? Thirdly, how did he get there? It was almost like he was at the right place at the right time to receive his blessing. Did God lead this blind man here? Possibly. In our Christian walk, if we allow God to lead our path, He will lead us to places to receive blessings.

A Crowd: What Were They Doing Here?

In verses 36 and 37, we learn that Jesus and a multitude of people passed by. If this was to be a simple miracle, why didn't Jesus and a couple of disciples pass by? And who were these multitudes of people? Disciples? Newly converted Christians or just spectators looking for a magic show? Whoever they were, we discover in verse 43, that everyone saw Jesus heal the blind man and gave praise to God. I believe the Lord uses people and their unfortunate circumstances for His glory. An example would be if a drug addict got saved. If everyone that knew him saw his transformation, they would know where it came from and the Lord would get the glory for it. Many lives would be touched. Wouldn't they?

Jesus, Can You Hear Me?
In verses 38 and 39, the blind man calls out to Jesus not once, but twice. Did Jesus not hear him the first time? Was Jesus deaf? I think there are lessons to learn here. One is being persistent in our requests to God.

In I Thessalonians 5:17, it tells us to pray without ceasing. I think as Christians we need to continually make our requests known to God until He answers. Another important lesson in these two verses is the fact that this blind man was told basically to 'shut up' by people from the crowd. That didn't stop him from calling out to Jesus again. That's pretty bold, don'tcha think? I think the Lord wants us to be bold in our prayers to Him. Proverbs 28:1 says that the righteous are as bold as a lion.

Who Are You Telling To Hush?
Why did some of the people from the crowd tell the blind man to keep his peace? From what I read in John 9:2, people believed that the blind were cursed this way because of their sin or the sin of their parents. I imagine everyone thought this blind man was a bad person because of his disability.

They didn't even want him to speak. He was being judged by those around him. Are we as critical of others? Do we judge someone because of the way they appear?

Remember, Jesus can save anybody!

The Blind Walk Of Faith
The blind man didn't address Jesus as 'Jesus of Nazareth'. He addressed Him as Jesus 'Son of David'. There's a big difference here. By calling Him the Son of David, he knew that this was the promised Messiah that the prophets spoke of long ago. This was his Lord! The blind man was also brought to Jesus. He took the steps of faith to receive his blessing. We should be walking in faith, too.

A Servant Spirit
The amazing words of Jesus is found right here in verse 41. Jesus asks the blind man simply, "What can I do for you?" Can you imagine the scene? A helpless blind man comes to Jesus looking for help and Jesus is ready and willing to help this guy out. To me, that's awesome. Jesus is ready and willing to help us in our times of need, too. All we have to do is come to Him and ask.

I Was Blind, But Now I See
In verse 42, the blind man receives his sight. Jesus heals him. I believe this symbolizes a lost sinner that doesn't know Jesus as Lord and Savior. The day will come when they will realize that they are 'blind' and need Jesus in their life to make them 'see'. A whole new world will open up to them and see things that they have never seen before. It's an awesome feeling! It's a powerful scripture when you dig into it and analyze things closer.

Jesus Heals a Centurion's Boy of Palsy
Matthew 8: 5-13

Now that's a lot of reading! It could easily be accepted as another miraculous healing produced from faith in Jesus. I believe there is more to it than that.

Let's look at the characters involved: Jesus, a centurion, a servant of a centurion, and followers.

A centurion was a career military officer in the Roman army that had many officers under them. These guys were hated by the Jews because of their power over them. This particular centurion pushed aside these obstacles in order to come to Jesus - his pride, doubt, money, language, distance, time, self-sufficiency, power, and race. This amazed the Lord about this centurion's faith! This pertains to us because these are the same things that can come between us and the Lord if we let them. We need to let go of these things when it comes to serving or requesting anything from Jesus.

What keeps you from Him?
Another thing that stands out to me is the fact that the centurion came to Jesus on behalf of one of his servants. He was concerned with the well-being of someone else. He wasn't 'all about me'. We should be the same way. We should be praying for people around us and stop focusing all of our prayer time on our own needs. Let's serve others like Jesus would!

In verses 11 and 12, Jesus speaks to His followers of the gathering of people from the east and the west to sit down with Abraham, Isaac and Jacob in the kingdom of heaven. The east and the west generally means all four corners of the earth. Considering the centurion was a Gentile, I believe this gathering includes both the Jews and the Gentiles. I believe that in these passages, the Jews considered themselves 'children of the kingdom' not because of their faith in the Lord but because of who they were - Jews. They felt that because they were Jews that it guaranteed their place in the Kingdom. Jesus tells us that heaven is for both Jews and Gentiles. According to these verses, many will be cast out into outer darkness. It's a real place and many will be going there!

This tells me that our works won't save us! It's not our role in our religious ceremonies that will save us. It's not who we are - it about the One on the throne! We can only be saved through faith in Jesus Christ! We need to humble ourselves before the Lord in prayer and ask Him to come into our lives.

It's not about religion - it's about a relationship with our Lord and Savior, Jesus Christ! Time is running out folks and we need to quit playing games! The Lord is coming back soon and we need to be ready! Are you saved? Do you know Jesus as Lord and Savior of your life? If not, you may want to make things right! Take the step today!

Jesus Heals a Dumb Man
Matthew 9: 32-35

This is the only place that this particular miracle is presented. It's an awesome thing that Jesus did for this man. Even though it doesn't say how Jesus healed him, whether through a word or a touch, it is still a great miracle because of how the people reacted to it. They marveled! They were surprised, amazed, and became curious! It says that they had never before seen this in Israel. It must have been an amazing thing that happened right before their eyes.

There is something strange to me about this miracle when you compare it to the others mentioned in the Bible. It doesn't say that the healed man 'followed' Jesus afterward. It doesn't say that the multitude that was watching in amazement 'followed' Jesus after the miracle happened. Normally, a person or crowd would follow Jesus or run off and tell others of the great thing that Jesus had done. It didn't happen this time. Isn't that kind of strange?

However, it does end with a group of people, called Pharisees, making a critical comment about Jesus and the miracle. They basically tell the crowd that it was the work of the devil. Who were these people? From what I have read, they were like the latest 'movement' or 'popular fad' in those days. Their rules and regulations were popular among the Jews. Christianity was something new and the whole 'Jesus thing' didn't fit in with their way of life. Doesn't that sound like the world today? Many people have pushed the Lord out of their lives. Our country has pushed Him out of our culture. We know He exists and we know of all of the great things He has done, but we choose to remain 'silent' because He's not 'popular' in our existing world. Many Christians today do not 'speak' because they are afraid of being ridiculed or rejected by others.

This is especially true among Christian teenagers today. If they were to start talking 'Jesus stuff' among their friends, they would be considered an outcast. Rejected! So instead, they choose to remain 'silent' and do not witness to others. It's safer and much easier. They can be Christians and still keep their friends. Right?

That's not how it's supposed to be. We have a responsibility as a

Christian and that is to tell the world of how great our Lord is. Put aside culture, popularity, and selfish reasoning. People need to know about Jesus! You have a voice and you need to be heard! Get rid of that demon that's keeping you silent.

Jesus Heals a Leper
Matthew 8: 1-4

Leprosy was a serious disease back in the days when Jesus walked the Earth. There was no cure - no skilled doctors, antibiotics, or fancy hospitals. People with leprosy had to walk around in their designated areas, away from people, while their skin rotted off. It was terrible! If they came in contact with someone, this person could catch their disease. I believe leprosy mentioned in the Bible represents sin. Sin is very similar in that it rots us to the core. It isolates us from a relationship with the Lord. It separates us from the glory of God in our life. We walk around with this disease and it rubs off on others. Sin will eventually lead to death!

It says in verse 1 that Jesus came down from the mountain with a multitude of people. This meant the leper was down in the valley. That's kind of ironic. Weren't we in the valley when Jesus met us? I think some of us would call it 'rock bottom'. Thank you Jesus for coming down to save me! Amen?

The leper asked (prayed), "Lord, if you will, you can make me whole." His faith knew that the Lord COULD heal him, but he didn't know if He WOULD. Keep in mind, this leper had a contagious disease. Anyone near him could have caught what he had. Jesus could have easily said out loud from the mountain, "Be clean!" and he would have been healed. But, no! He reached out and touched him in the condition he was in right then and there. Many people think they are too far gone in their sin and that no one can save them. Let me tell you...YOU'RE WRONG!!

I know someone that can - His name is Jesus! Don't be ashamed of where you are and don't run from the Lord's mercy. Run to Him! He can and will heal you if you let Him!

I'm not sure of why Jesus didn't want the leper to tell anyone that he had been healed. I imagine He didn't want a crowd. Personally, it's hard to keep quiet when the Lord does a work in your life. We don't have an excuse. The Lord has already told us to tell everyone the things He has done in our life. Are we a walking testimony? Are we telling others?

Jesus Heals Peter's Mother-Inlaw
Matthew 8: 14, 15

Hmm... interesting. This woman that Jesus healed had a fever. Was it life threatening? The Bible doesn't say. I would assume that since she was 'laid' meant it was bad enough for her to be in bed and she probably didn't feel like getting up and moving around. Her illness wasn't as bad as some of the other healings Jesus performed - leprosy, blindness, deafness, and raising the dead.

Who are the characters? Let's see: Jesus, Peter, and his mother-in-law. After reading from the Internet on Peter, it tells me that Peter was one of the Twelve Apostles that Jesus chose to be one of His disciples. He was a fisherman by trade.

The Roman Catholic Church considers Peter to be a saint. Also, according to

Catholic tradition, Peter was the first bishop of Rome and Catholics argue that the Pope is Peter's successor and therefore rank superior of all other bishops. In church tradition, Peter is said to have founded the church in Rome (along with Paul).

According to sources from the Internet, the Roman Catholic Church (officially known as the Catholic Church) is the world's largest Christian Church representing over half of all Christians and one-sixth of the world's population. The Church looks to the Pope as its highest supreme authority in matters of faith, morality and Church governance. If the Pope is Peter's successor and if Peter founded the Catholic Church, then the Church would govern based on the teachings of Peter inspired by Jesus. Right?

Here's where I have questions. If married men can 'only' be deacons of the Catholic Church, why can 'only' celibate (not married) men become ordained as priests when the Bible plainly says that Peter (the founder of the Catholic Church) was married? By omitting this simple fact, could it affect the way the Catholic Church is run?

Another thing I discovered is that homosexuals can be ordained as deacons if followed by three years of prayer and chastity. Does this mean that they have to repent of their sin of homosexuality or that being homosexual is OK and all they need to do is pray for three years and abstain from sexual activity? I imagine if any kind of sin is allowed in a church, it will affect the whole church and its mission for Christ. It would be like putting a rotten apple in a basket of good ones. It's going to mess it up!

I do not claim to be a scholar nor have the knowledge needed in this subject. I am not trying to attack any church and/or their beliefs. I can only say that the Bible states that Peter was married. I would encourage you to study and dig deeper into this. Pray for the Lord to give you understanding. I believe there is more to these two verses than just a woman getting healed of a simple fever.

Jesus Restores Sight to a Blind Man

Mark 8: 22-26

This particular miracle baffled me. At first glance, it seemed that Jesus had some miracle working struggles. It was as if His power was weakening. Instead of healing with a single touch or spoken word, this miracle of receiving sight took two attempts. What is up with that? Let's look a little closer.

We learn that Jesus was in the town of Bethsaida. As I discovered from the book of Matthew (chapter 11, verses 21 - 24), Bethsaida was a place where Jesus had performed many miracles. The problem in this town is the people saw Him do the miracles, but

they refused to repent of their sins and refused to believe. Knowing that, then this miracle in Mark 8:22-26 is basically a miracle of 'seeing is believing'. This blind man had a problem - he couldn't see! This tells me that he was blind to spiritual truth. He was brought to Jesus for a special healing - a miracle.

Jesus knew the town of Bethsaida and He knew its people. He knew that they had seen His miracles before and still didn't believe. He also knew that part of this man's blindness was caused by him fitting in with the people around him. The man needed a change in environment.

Jesus takes him away from the village and begins working the miracle. The change of environment put him in a position of a 'one on one' relationship with Him. No distractions! It's easier to focus when your eyes are on the right things. Now, here comes the touch.

Jesus spit and touched the man. This should have been enough to heal the man. It was almost like Jesus was giving the man spiritual 'baby steps'. The man received partial vision. He was able to see a little better. After Jesus touched him, He asked the man, "What do you see?" The man looks up and replies by saying, "I see people. They look like trees walking around." I'm sure the man's faith was increasing at this point and wasn't content with the partial healing. I imagine he wanted more and believed that Jesus could do it.

Jesus touched the man's eyes a second time. This touch fully restored the man's vision. He could see completely. Jesus leaves him with a warning, "Don't go into the village."

What's the message here for us?

For me, there are two. One is for the Christian and the other for those that don't know Jesus as their Lord and Savior.

If you are saved, are you spiritually walking in the town of Bethsaida? You have seen Jesus perform miracles in your life and in the lives of others. When problems come to you, why do you doubt that Jesus will see you through? He has done it before, He will do it again. Is your response to life's problems followed by stress and worry? Don't worry - just believe!

If you have never accepted Jesus as Savior, why not? You have seen how He has changed the lives of others around you. People have talked to you about Jesus and have invited you to church, but you still don't want any part of it. Why? Do these people look like 'walking trees' to you? You are blind to spiritual truth. Allow Jesus to come into your life and open your eyes.

Jesus wants you to know Him. It may take you stepping out of your 'Bethsaida' to do it. And if you decide to step out, don't go back. Keep your focus on Him.

Raising of a Widow's Son at Nain
Luke 7: 11-16

Jesus, many of His disciples, and several people entered into the city gates of Nain. As soon as they arrived, they noticed a man being carried out either in a casket or a stretcher. The man was dead! Jesus saw a woman crying. The dead man was her only son. To make matters worse, she was already a widow. I would assume that her husband had passed away, too. Her world was crashing down all around her. What was she going to do?

Jesus had compassion and brought her son back to life. The mother and the son probably lived happily ever after. This was a sweet story, but what was the meaning behind it all?

One of the things that stood out to me was that the widow woman didn't come to Jesus in search of a miracle. Jesus came to her. This is very different than all of the previous miracles before. Why did Jesus help this family? What was it about this family that made Jesus reach out?

It could be said that He was showing the people that He was a great prophet. The only great prophets they knew at the time were Elijah and Elisha. Both of these people had performed a miracle such as bringing the dead to life, but they were long gone. Maybe Jesus wanted to show them who He was.

Maybe the miracle was symbolic for what was going to come; Jesus' death and resurrection. Maybe everyone needed to see this miracle to know that He could do it again. It could have been the faith builder they needed when they would see Him on the cross.

Or maybe, just maybe, this miracle was to show everyone a character of Jesus. He had a love for people and cared enough for them to reach out even though they didn't.

Here's the deal. This widow was hanging on by a string. Her husband had died and now her son. Where was her income going to come from? She would have been all alone to support herself. A situation like this could have put her on the street. She may have become a beggar or even worse. It could be that this dead man had a purpose in life to serve the Lord. Who knows the outcome of this situation? Jesus did. That's why He stepped in to help.

Jesus still does this today. How many times has your destructive road took an unsuspected detour? For many of us, how many times have situations changed that should have left you dead? Ever wonder why you are still here?

Jesus knows your past, present, and future. He knows you have a purpose – His purpose. Are you living for Him? If not, you need to be. He has a plan – and you're in it. Pray and find out what it is.

Raising Of Lazarus
John 11: 1-45

That was a lot of reading, but it has a message to all of us. It was indeed a great miracle. No doubt! But it was one with a delayed reaction. Out of all of the miracles that Jesus performed, this may be the one that most people will remember. Why? I think it's because everyone can relate to it. Here we have a man that is dying. His name is Lazarus and he is real sick. His sisters, Mary and Martha, get a word out to Jesus who is ministering in another town to come and heal their brother. It's an emergency! 911 – Hello!!

Jesus loved this family and was close to them, but His reaction time was delayed. Did He truly care? Did He just say that He loved them and not really mean it? After hearing the news, He stayed in the town that He was ministering in for two more days. Why didn't He leave when He heard about His friend's serious illness? He could've prevented his death!

After reading all of these verses, I realized there were several people involved in this miracle. There were Mary, Martha, and Lazarus in the beginning. Of course, there were Jesus and His disciples. But after Lazarus died, several Jews got involved. Jesus could have spoken a word and healed Lazarus when he was sick, but because of His delay, many people witnessed the miracle of bringing Lazarus from the grave and began following Him. It was like Jesus used the 'delay' to bring in a larger crowd. This miracle would have a bigger purpose than a simple 'helping a friend out' miracle. Are you with me?

When preachers preach on this miracle, the main point is that Jesus was four days late, but He was right on time. This may be hard to believe, but God's timing is perfect. It may not seem perfect to us, but we have to look outside the box. In this case, His timing meant everything! By waiting, more lives were touched and they became followers.

What prayers are you waiting for to be answered today? It may seem like its too late, but what if it's not? What if the Lord is waiting for the right precise moment to give it to you? It could be the time when everyone around you is watching - an audience. And at that precise moment, the miracle touches their life and they become saved through it. Wouldn't the wait be worth it? Think about it!

Your prayer + your waiting time + your miracle = their life restored to God, or better yet, their salvation! Now that's awesome stuff right there! In every miracle Jesus performed, there was always someone watching.

In your miracle, maybe He's waiting for the audience.

Raising The Ruler's Daughter

Matthew 9: 18-26

One of the first things I noticed by reading this scripture is the fact that there are two miracles that seemed to happen all at once. Even though there are two miracles, I am going to discuss only one of them even though I believe they are somehow linked together with a spiritual meaning. Let's take a look:

Who are the characters in this scripture? Jesus, a ruler, a dead daughter, a bleeding woman, and a crowd. All needing a miracle in their life - well, except for Jesus of course. It begins with a ruler coming to Jesus with a serious situation. His daughter was dying! He had the faith that the Lord could heal her by the touch of His hand. This kind of faith got Jesus' attention and proceeded to follow the ruler back to his home. We could say right here that this ruler, with all of his leadership skills, knew who the true leader of his life was. He could have taken charge of the situation on his own.

Many of us like to be in control of every situation. When we pray for something, we even like to be in control of how the prayer will be answered.

"Lord, I need You to answer my prayer this way - MY way."

"Lord, if you will answer my prayer like this, it will work out for the best."

If we really want the Lord to lead our life, we need to step back with Jesus in the front leading and guiding the way.

As the Lord followed the ruler back to his home, Jesus stopped and helped someone else. This guy's daughter was dying! It

was an emergency that needed Jesus right away! Why is He stopping to help someone else? The bleeding woman could wait! She had been bleeding for twelve years. I'm sure another day wouldn't hurt. Haha! Sound familiar? Do you get jealous when you see other people's prayers getting answered while you're still waiting for yours? I believe there is a lesson here. We need to rejoice when the Lord works in other people's lives and to understand that the Lord hasn't forgotten about us. It could be His way of helping us to get rid of our sense of self-centeredness; our 'all about me' way of thinking.

The Lord finally arrived at the ruler's house, but it was too late. His daughter was dead. The people were gathered for the funeral ceremony. The musicians were there, too. I guess they had already given up on Jesus. Since He never arrived when they wanted Him to, they went ahead and prepared for the funeral. It was too late for the miracle, right? Jesus even told them it wasn't too late, but they laughed at Him. But as we read, we see that Jesus knew what He was doing. The dead girl 'arose' from the touch of Jesus. The crowd saw it and the news of the miracle spread throughout the land. This tells me that no problem is too big or beyond fixing. We may think it's too late for a miracle in our life. That's not the case! All we have to do is give it to the Lord and have faith in Him that He will fix it. Jesus can do miracles in our life that will amaze us.

We may think there is no hope, but let me tell you something. There is hope in my Lord and Savior. Give all of your cares to Him.

He IS the Great Physician! And He's a Carpenter, too. Let Him fix it!

Restoring a Servant's Ear

Luke 22: 49-51

This miracle is part of Jesus' betrayal by Judas when Jesus was arrested by the religious leaders.

Judas led the crowd to where Jesus and His disciples were and showed them who Jesus was by kissing Him. The disciples realized what was about to happen and asked Jesus, "Should we use our swords on them?" Before Jesus could answer, one of them draws his sword and cuts the ear off of one of the servants. John 18:10 says the man that did it was Simon Peter. But, Jesus had compassion for the servant and restored his ear. End of story...right? This was a great miracle for the servant and the one's that saw it, but was there a purpose or meaning behind it? Let's take a closer look:

Jesus and His disciples were in a place called Mount of Olives. Judas was missing. Jesus was speaking to them and telling them not to fall into temptation. He was also full of sorrow and prayed, that if it was God's will, that He would take this cup from Him. The disciples were also sad. It was like they knew something bad was going to happen. After He finished praying, Jesus went back to the disciples and found them sleeping. He told them to wake up and pray so that they would not fall into temptation.

The next thing you know, a crowd shows up. Judas was ahead of the crowd and walks up to Jesus and kisses Him. Now we have a strange scene with two opposing forces. Jesus and the disciples on one side and religious leaders and a crowd that wants to arrest Jesus on the other. This is like a scene of 'saved' versus 'unsaved'. The saved are about to be persecuted. What should they do?

Peter steps up to the plate and draws his sword. The ironic thing to me about this is that, in the Bible, it describes the Word of God as a sword (Ephesians 6:17, Hebrews 4:12). What if this was another lesson in ministry? Picture this scenario:

The disciples were surrounded by unsaved people and they were persecuting them. Peter pulls out his Bible and begins ministering. His approach was not in a loving Christian way. Peter, without thinking, attacks one of them with the scriptures, not out of love and compassion, but with anger. This attack cuts this person's ear off, not physically, but spiritually. This person had lost his ability to hear the Word because of the way it was presented. It did more harm than good. Jesus, out of love and compassion for this lost man, restores his ear - his hearing. Which of these two approaches would lead the man to a personal relationship with Jesus?

I believe the message is clear and it's one of discipleship and ministry. It is so easy to attack someone that is lost with the Word of God. Our motive may be an attempt to lead them to Jesus, but we use tactics that attack them as a person instead of their sin. The problem is that this approach cuts their ears off and makes them not want to hear the Word or anything you got to say. We actually do more harm than good and basically drive them further away.

If we minister like Jesus' example, we would be more concerned with the person's well-being, and out of love, we would focus more on their sin. By doing so, this person would be more open to 'hear' the Word and be open to 'want' a relationship with Jesus.

The Word of God has power! The power is within itself, not the user that applies it. Our job is to share it with others, not to use it to attack someone!

There are many people out there that need to hear it. If we use it as a weapon, the result will be destructive. Jesus says, "No more of this!"

Let's minister out of love and compassion to the lost - just as Jesus did.

Second Draught of Fish
John 21: 1-14

The interesting thing to me from this miracle is not that Jesus showed the disciples where the 'big catch of the day' was, but it was the fact that this was the second time Jesus finds Peter back at his boat fishing after he had decided to follow Him.

Read these scriptures for more details: Matthew 4: 18-20 and Luke 5: 1-11

What was Peter doing back at his boat? Did he give up on his ministry? The sad thing is that he took other disciples with him - six to be exact. It sounds like he could have been worried about money issues and chose to use his time in his business instead of doing the 'free' work in ministry or maybe he felt ministry was too complicated and just gave up. The simple message from this would be to stay focused on what the Lord is telling you to do. If you are in a God-called ministry, remain in there, don't worry about anything, and let God take care of the details. I mentioned this in another message:

Draught of Fish (Luke 5: 1-11)

Could this be a similar message? Or is there more? The more I read into this, a few things stood out to me like a sore thumb. The scripture mentions they caught some fish. A hundred and fifty three (153) to be exact! Isn't that an odd number? Why (153) fish? Did someone really take the time to count? If so, why?

It tells us that Peter jumped out of the boat when he saw that it was Jesus. The other disciples followed behind pulling the net filled with fish. They were only two hundred cubits away. This is the equivalence of 300 feet (100 yards). I know this because I looked it up. The number here is two hundred (200).

It also mentions that this was the third time Jesus visited the disciples after He was raised from the dead. The number here is three (3). And the number of disciples that were present at the boat was seven (7).

Another interesting fact is that this miracle is the last recorded miracle out of the four Gospels. There is a lot going on here with this miracle with all of these numbers and the unfortunate thing is that my brain can't comprehend it all. I know the Bible contains numbers and each has a special meaning. I did a search on the internet and uncovered many websites concerning these numbers and their possible meanings. There are studies of numbers called Theomatics and Gematria. These are worth checking into. Do a search for yourself.

Here are some cool facts that I found on the Internet:
1. In the KJV of the Bible, Peter's name is mentioned 153 times.
2. In the KJV of the Bible, Paul's name is mentioned 153 times.
3. It was believed in the Bible days, there were exactly 153 types of fish.
4. Over a century ago, a man made a discovery that there were exactly 153 people specifically blessed by Jesus. Most of these were in His miracles in the New Testament. His name was Lt. Col. R. Roberts (from Grant Jeffrey's book Unveiling Mysteries of the Bible).
5. It was thought the 153 fish represented the current number of nations that would receive the Gospel in those days.
6. I am sure there are more that you will find.

John, the disciple, was an interesting man from the Bible. He was the writer for a few of the books that bear his name, plus he wrote the book of Revelation. I believe his writings have a prophetic message to us. As we already know, the book of Revelation tells us of the things to come until Jesus returns and the world ends. Would the book of John be any different? I don't know.

In Revelation, it speaks of a time when people won't be able to buy or sell unless they had the mark of the beast (666) and everything would be under the control of some kind of world power. Knowing that made me think.

What organization do we have in the world today that controls how we do business? After doing some research, I found one called the World Trade

Organization (WTO). These guys are like a world government and they have a lot of power and their members include 95% of all the nations in the world. It originally started after World War II and was called General Agreement on Tariffs and Trade (GATT) and in 1982 it had some problems and WTO was created. WTO follows the same guidelines as GATT. It's like a secret government or something. Do a search on the Internet. It's pretty cool.

The thing that caught my attention on this subject was that on July 7, 2008, WTO received its 153rd member (Cape Verde). Also during this same time frame, the world enters an economic recession. Was this miracle a prophetic message of things to come? Or was John just bored and decided to count some fish? I believe all of these numbers (3, 7, 200, and 153) from this scripture have some significant meaning.

Unfortunately, I don't have the answers. We need to take the time in prayer and research to discover it.

Temple Tax in the Fish's Mouth

Matthew 17: 24-27

When I first read this, it didn't sound like a legitimate miracle. It came across as an attempt to bail out on paying taxes or Jesus using His miracle working powers to provide the means to pay them. This just didn't settle right with me so I began to study deeper into this.

What was this tribute money and who were these guys collecting it?

Based on what I've learned, the tribute money was a payment required of the Jewish males to pay to the temple. The temple and this money was a law established between God and Moses many years back. These guys that confronted Peter were appointed collectors for the temple.

Here's the question that Jesus gave to Peter, "Where do the kings of the earth get their tribute money? From their sons or from strangers?" Peters answer was 'strangers'. Jesus stated that this would make the sons exempt. This was a question of authority. The temple was setup for God, the Father. Jesus is His Son. Therefore, He would have been exempt, but the temple rulers did not recognize Him as the Son of God. In addition, if the Jews were inherited into the family of God, shouldn't they have been exempt, too? This tells me that being part of God's family involves a personal relationship instead of 'being a chosen breed'. Being a Jew doesn't guarantee you a special spot in God's family. It's when you repent and ask Jesus to come into your life.

Jesus could have stood His ground and presented His authority, but He chose not to offend them and decided to pay the tribute for both of them. This showed His humbleness and respect for authority even if they were wrong.

He sent Peter out to the sea to go fishing. Peter was an experienced fisherman and was used to spreading out nets to catch several fish, but it sounds like Jesus sent Him out with a fishing pole and a hook. Jesus told him that that the first fish he caught would have the tribute money in its mouth. It sounded like a simple task. Jesus could have had a bag of money fall from the sky or could have pulled it out of Peter's ear like a magician. What was the purpose of all of this?

Whenever Jesus performed a miracle, it always had a deeper meaning than what it first appeared. We could easily say that Jesus can provide the possible when it seems impossible. We could also say that Jesus' miracle working power goes beyond the realm of the natural and even affects nature. If you think about it, what are the chances of the first fish you catch having money in its mouth? That's pretty amazing!

The 'fish' seems to be a symbolism of the Christian faith. Jesus fed the 5000 and the 4000 people fish and bread. The early persecuted Christians would use the fish symbol on their homes to let other Christians know that it was safe to come there and worship. Even today, the symbol is used on bumper stickers for our cars and even in businesses to let other know that we are Christians.

Could it be that the tribute money represented the price of salvation to become sons and daughter of God? The Jews were paying it as part of the law. But for Christians, the price has already been paid and that Jesus provided it on the cross.

When Peter pulled that fish (representing his Christianity) out of the water, it didn't cost him anything. His tribute money had already been furnished by Jesus when he opened the fish's mouth.

The Healing Of a Paralytic
Matthew 9: 1-8

Palsy is the inability to move. This man was brought to Jesus lying in a bed and was paralyzed. He couldn't move! His crippling disease kept him from doing the things that normal people could do. But Jesus healed him by saying, "Be of good cheer! Your sins are forgiven!" Wait a minute. Let's stop right there!

There's more to this, right?

If I had to guess, I would say that this man was paralyzed by sin. Not that he committed a sin that caused him to have palsy, but it symbolizes that he was paralyzed in his heart. He felt guilty, at fault, to blame, wicked, ashamed, and self-condemning for the sins that he had committed. Guilt is crippling. It can alter your personality and relationships. It can erode your self-image and sap your morale.

When Jesus said this to the man with palsy, the scribes didn't know what to think. They thought Jesus was blaspheming God. They didn't know that He was God in the flesh before their very eyes. But Jesus revealed His power to them and to us on earth that He has the power to forgive sins. This is a confirmation to us that when we ask the Lord in prayer to forgive us and are living according to His will, our sins are forgiven. He has the power to do it! The message today is this:

You may be living in guilt and are feeling depressed about something you may have done in your past. It might be that you had an affair or you were promiscuous at some point in your history. Nobody knows about it, but the guilt of it is affecting your marriage or your relationships. It might be you had an abortion and almost no one knows of it, but the guilt of it is affecting your life. Only you and the Lord knows what you are holding inside that's paralyzing you spiritually.

When Jesus died on the cross, He died for ALL of your sins. Give it to Him and ask for forgiveness! You can be assured because:

He will say, "Be of good cheer! Your sins are forgiven!" You won't be paralyzed anymore.

Turning Water into Wine

John 2: 1-11

After reading this, it sounds at first like a 'drunken' party. People are gathered around celebrating, getting 'wasted' and having a great time. Jesus and His disciples were there, too. The party almost comes to an end and it creates a serious dilemma - they have ran out of 'booze'.

This reminds me of my old partying days; drinking and hanging out with my friends. When the alcohol was gone, we had two choices. We could end the party and go home or we could send someone out on a 'beer run' and get more. The verses above seems like Jesus was called to make the dash for more 'juice'. This isn't

the Jesus that I know and doesn't settle with me knowing how He had delivered me years ago from this act of self-destruction. We need to look at this a little closer:

Verses like this is used in religious debates on whether it's OK to drink or not. In people's minds they think if Jesus is willing to turn water into wine, then it's OK to drink and get drunk. I have my own personal convictions on this subject and don't plan to push them on anyone. Everyone that is saved has their own relationship with the Lord. The Holy Spirit will let that individual know whether it's OK to drink or not. I believe the 'wine' mentioned in the verses is used to represent spiritual matters.

There was a celebration going on - a Jewish celebration. Someone was getting married. As part of the Jewish traditions, when a person got married, it was a 'new life' for them. They would invite the whole town and would celebrate for a week. It was also an insult to refuse an invitation to the party. Everybody was there. I believe the reason Jesus and His disciples attended was because of the opportunity He had to minister to a larger crowd. Yes, wine was served. But, understand, this was part of their Jewish tradition and to run out of it broke their unwritten law of hospitality. It was also embarrassing for the ones giving the party. So, this did create a problem for them.

Jesus was called upon to do a miracle. He had to produce some 'wine' and He used some of their tools to do it - six stone water jars and water.

The stone water jars were used by the Jews for ceremonial purposes. A Jew that sinned that day could walk up and 'wash' his hands from the jar filled with water and become 'clean' again. It was an exterior cleansing. It's interesting to know that Jesus used the same jars to fill with His 'new' wine for them to drink 'internally'.

He told them to serve the master of the banquet. They did and the master of the banquet shared it with the bridegroom and said, "Everyone brings out the choice wine first and then the cheaper wine after the guests have had too much to drink; but you have saved the best till now." Sounds to me like they were more than satisfied.

So, what's this all about?

I believe the wine represents 'spirituality'. The Jews were and are religious people. They knew the laws that were given to them by Moses from God. They held religious ceremonies, gathered in synagogues and 'walked' by their religion. The sad thing is that they didn't know who Jesus was. They were drinking 'wine', but their 'wine' would run out and come up empty. They would also offer the choice wine at first and resort to a 'cheaper wine' when they had their fill. Jesus offered a 'new wine' - the best for last. The wine He offered worked better when they discovered that theirs had run out and left them empty. Is this a message of 'to drink' or 'not to drink'?

No, it's a spiritual message of 'where are you drinking from?' Are you practicing a religion that's leaving you filling empty? Has your religion really changed and 'cleansed' your life? Jesus is saving the 'best for last' for you today!

Drink from the well that never runs dry! Accept Jesus into your life and experience a 'one on one' relationship with Him today! Drink up!!

Walking On the Sea

Matthew 14: 23-33

I have heard sermons preached on these verses from Matthew. It seems to be a message on faith and how we as Christians should put all of our trust in the Lord. Peter's faith was tested when he took the step out of the boat and began walking on the water. As long as he had his eyes on the Lord he could walk towards Jesus, but when he looked away and focused on the storm around him, instead of Jesus, he began to sink. This is a true message for us in our Christian walk, but is this the only message from these verses?

Not today!

According to the Bible, this is about the fifteenth miracle the disciples witnessed Jesus perform. At this point, they still had nearly twenty-two more to see and Jesus was gradually revealing more of Himself to them. As you look back on the previous miracles, you know that Jesus was a miracle worker that healed sicknesses in people's lives and provided for people's needs. The disciples realized that Jesus was a physician and a provider. I imagine they were comfortable with that.

These disciples were in a boat on the sea a few miles from the shore. Jesus was on dry land on a mountain praying by Himself. These disciples did not have Jesus with them at this time. While they were in the boat, a storm was brewing. The winds were blowing strong and their boat was being tossed around. A couple of these guys were fisherman and knew about storms on the water, so I don't think they were scared of it and I'm sure they knew how to handle the boat. The fear came when they saw Jesus coming toward them on the water. They didn't realize it was Him. They thought He was a ghost! This was something they hadn't seen Him do before! This was something new to them. Peter was the only one that stepped out on faith. I believe he looked back on all that Jesus had done and was willing to see what Jesus could do in this new environment on the sea. I think Peter wanted to experience this new power that Jesus wanted to reveal to them. He wanted to know more about His Lord. So, he took a walk on the water!

As long as he focused his mind and thoughts on Jesus, he was able to get closer to Him. But, when he started looking around and began getting distracted with his surroundings, he would sink.

There is a lesson in all of this. Being a Christian to me is about a personal relationship with Jesus Christ. It's not about a religious experience. Religion is made up of 'dos' and 'don'ts' and ceremonial routines. This separates us from the relationship that Jesus would like to have with us.

Who is Jesus to you? What do you know about Him? Is He just the character you read about in the Bible stories or the man depicted in the low budget movies you see around Christmas time? The real question is how much would you like to know about Him?

Being 'in the boat' could represent our Christianity. We could continue to remain comfortable where we are and never experience everything Jesus has to offer. Or we could step outside of the 'religion box' and walk on the water towards a closer relationship with our Lord.

You may think every time you face a 'storm' that it's just a test of faith to see if you trust Jesus to see you through. It could be Jesus trying to reveal Himself to you by showing you who He is during the 'storm'.

Step out of the boat and walk closer to Him. You may learn something new.

Withering the Fig Tree
Matthew 21: 18, 19

It sounds like Jesus got mad at a tree and made it die. For what? Because it didn't have figs on it? That would be a selfish and thoughtless thing to do, wouldn't you think? This doesn't sound like the character of Jesus Christ. There must be more to this than what we are reading. Let's dig deeper!

Jesus was hungry! He came across a fig tree and noticed that there weren't any figs on the tree. From a distance, it looked fruitful because it had leaves. But, the closer He looked into it, the leaves were the only thing that it had. No figs - no fruit - no food! That's discouraging!

I believe the fig tree represents religion; religion in the Christian church and in Christian people. I feel that Jesus was disgusted with the fact that no fruit was coming forth from it. Even though it had an outward appearance of growth, it had no fruit.

Fruit in the Church
As Christians, we get spiritually hungry. We need to receive the Word of God as part of our spiritual diet to survive. Reading the Bible and going to church is how we receive this nourishing fruit (food).

Many churches give the outward appearance of a fruitful place to receive spiritual nourishment, but when we get inside, it's as 'dead as a door nail'. We walk out of the church feeling the same way we did before we went in there.

Big churches and small churches can fall into this category. If your church has turned into a social club and is not preaching the Word of God, then this message is for you! I believe a church that is Holy Spirit filled is one that you will feel when you go through the doors.

Church, forget about the numbers in attendance and forget about pleasing the members! Preach the Word! Pray for a revival and allow the Holy Spirit to work in you and through you. Then, you will begin seeing the fruit in your church and in its congregation. Your members will be fed and people will get saved!

Fruit in a Christian
There are a lot of Christian people out there that's not growing spiritually. They have been content with 'just being saved'. Jesus wants to see fruit in you!

He wants to see changes in your life and He wants to see your 'new' life bearing fruit in others.

What have you done for Jesus lately? Are you spreading His Word? Are you telling others about Him? Why not?

Yes, you may be showing the outward appearance of a Christian by going to church regularly and attending the 'church functions'. But, how do you act in the world? This is where you put your faith in action. This is the mission field! If you act 'like Jesus' during the week like you do on Sunday, you will start seeing fruit and the lives of people around you will change.

Quit sitting still! We should always be about our Father's business by leading others to Him. You have a job to do - spread the Word! Look at all of those people around you that don't know Jesus as Lord and Savior. How many more times are you going to let them pass you by before you say something to them?

Tell them about Jesus!

This is the message for us today: BE FRUITFUL!! Get back into the Word of God and start living the life that Jesus intended for you to live!

The Parables of Jesus Christ

The Four Soils
Luke 8: 5-8

This is the second parable mentioned in the book of Luke. It sounds like a story about a farmer planting a garden and throwing his seeds in four areas on the ground. I'm sure the farmer's intentions were to grow a healthy crop, but it appears that some of the choices he made of where to plant his seeds weren't good ones.

What would this mean to us? I'm not a farmer. I've tried growing simple things like tomatoes but have never been successful. I think we all know this parable isn't a guide for farming or to provide helpful plant growing tips.

Jesus explains the meaning in the later verses:

Now the parable is this: The seed is the word of God. Those by the way side are they that hear; then cometh the devil, and taketh away the word out of their hearts, lest they should believe and be saved. They on the rock are they, which, when they hear, receive the word with joy; and these have no root, which for a while believe, and in time of temptation fall away. And that which fell among thorns are they, which, when they have heard, go forth, and are choked with cares and riches and pleasures of this life, and bring no fruit to perfection. But that on the good ground are they, which in an honest and good heart, having heard the word, keep it, and bring forth fruit with patience. - Luke 8:11-15

Everyone will hear the Word of God. It doesn't matter who you are. Children of God are spreading the Good News everywhere. It could be in your neighborhood, at your job, or right here. If you are reading this, you are getting a dose of God's Word right now. The important thing is what you do with it after you hear it.

People represent the four soils. As individuals, we are one of them; a path, a rock, thorns, or good soil. Which one are you?

A Path

This is an unsaved person; someone that doesn't know Jesus as Lord and Savior. They could be an atheist or someone who practices some other religion that doesn't believe in the Living God.

If you fall into this category, you have heard about Jesus and His Word but you have chosen to push Him away. The devil has hardened your heart and filled your mind with doubts to the point where you don't want no part of it.

A Rock

This is someone that believes in God, but hasn't taken that step to ask for forgiveness and let Him into their life.

You could be the person that believes that God exists and you think that your 'good works' alone will save you. Wrong! Believing is not enough! That's not how it works! Just like planting on a rock, it doesn't root. A person has to be rooted in Jesus Christ and it begins with a relationship with Him.

Thorns

These people are saved. They have asked for forgiveness, but they do not let Jesus become the Lord of their life. They either allow the worries of life rule over them or they put their trust and time into the pleasures of the world. This includes money, material possessions, and sin. Bible reading, prayer, and going to church has been neglected and ranks at the bottom of their 'to do' list. Because of that, they are not growing as Christians.

If you are in this category, your spiritual life is in a mess. It shows in the way you act and in your home life. Being a Christian means to be 'Christ-like'. Are you living by His example?

Good Soil

This is the best category to be in. This is a person that has given their life to Jesus and is growing closer to Him everyday through His Word and prayer. He is number one in their life and it shows through the way they act and talk. Their life has meaning and they wake up with a sense of purpose. This person is a light in the world and Jesus is reflected through them for everyone to see.

If this is you, you will be producing a good crop. The Lord can use you to reach others. Lives around you will change because God is working through you. The fruits of the Spirit will fill your life: *love, joy, peace, patience, kindness, goodness, faithfulness, gentleness, and self control (Galatians 5:22, 23).*

Your life won't be easy because of the trials that you will face, but through each one, you will be molded to become more like Jesus. You are being who God wants you to be.

Take a look at yourself today. Which soil represents your life? I would hope you are in the right category by becoming good soil for the Lord.

The Weeds

Matthew 13:24-30

Jesus used farming in many of his parables because His disciples could relate to it. It was a common thing to do in those days. This is how they provided for themselves and their families. This parable speaks of sowing good seeds with the intent of producing a harvest. While in the midst, weeds are also planted by the enemy. As we already know, weeds can be a bad thing. Jesus explains the meaning in the following verses:

Read Matthew 13: 36-43

I know by reading these scriptures, the parable is self explanatory. Here's the deal! We are living in a sinful world today and the harvest is coming. We don't know when, but we are guaranteed that the time is drawing near. We are getting closer to it every day. If you are saved, it will be a day of rejoicing. If you don't know Jesus as Lord and Savior, your future isn't looking too good.

As Jesus says, He has sown some good seeds in the field; Christians living for Him in the world. Satan has done some sowing, too. The main point of this is to determine who you are and where you stand in the field. Who are you living for today?

If you are reading this, let this be your warning sign. It's time to wake up! Are you a 'good seed' planted by Jesus? Or are you a 'weed' in this world? While there is still time, I would evaluate your life and make sure you know for sure. Harvest time is coming folks! Don't get burned! Make Jesus the Lord of your life today!

The Mustard Seed

Matthew 13:31, 32

The mustard seed is known for being one of the smallest seeds that produces a large crop. The disciples knew this and that is why Jesus chose to use this parable as a way to describe the kingdom of Heaven.

It starts with Jesus!

For Christianity, it began when Jesus came to this Earth. He was considered 'small' in the eyes of the world. But, His words and example began to spread to others like the rippling effect on water and continues to grow today. By dying on the cross, He covered a multitude of sins - the sins of the world.

For Christians, it started the day we accepted Jesus into our lives. We didn't begin changing immediately, but as we desired to know more about Him and reached out to learn more from His Word, the transformation began to take place a little at a time. Every day is an opportunity for spiritual growth. By reading the Bible, praying, and going to church, we provide food for our soul (or fertilizer to the seed) that helps it grow.

The amazing thing about this growth is how it spreads to others. Our words and actions become a living testimony of how Jesus changed us. It's contagious! Some people are going to want it, too. Don't be surprised if they ask you how to receive it.

For unbelievers, a seed is planted in you, too. People have told you about Jesus and His free gift of salvation. You have heard about how He died on the cross for your sins. You also know that all you have to do is receive it by asking for forgiveness and accepting Jesus into your life. You have heard this before, right? If not, you are hearing it today!

What are you going to do with it? It's a seed planted within you and you have two choices. You can push it away like you have done many times before or you can act on it and watch it grow in your life. The choice is up to you!

The Yeast
Matthew 13:33

Here we have another comparison of what the kingdom of Heaven is like. It is being compared to yeast. I don't know how much you know about yeast, but all I know is that it somehow makes bread fluffy. So, I will need to do some research on this subject.

Wow! There's a lot of information on this subject, with scientific things and many big words that I can't pronounce. But, the main point is knowing what yeast does. When it is added to the mixture of bread, it gives it life and makes the bread rise. It's very similar to sticking your finger into an electric outlet and watching your hair turn into an afro. Just kidding! Do not try this at home! But, hopefully you get the idea.

If we were to think of our life as a slab of bread dough, the kingdom of Heaven as yeast, and if we add the two together, our life will spring up with some 'spiritual action'. We come alive! Things start happening! Are you hearing me? This is what the kingdom of Heaven is like folks! Jesus is the spark we have been looking for!

If you don't know Jesus as your Lord and Savior, you are basically a lump of 'flat' bread dough. It would be like making a bologna sandwich with pretzel sticks. It just doesn't work! You need some yeast in your bread!
Jesus tells us in John 6:48, *"I am that bread of life."* Accept Him into your life today!

The Treasure

Matthew 13:44

This parable of Jesus describes the kingdom of Heaven as a hidden treasure. I can't help but think of a pirate with a treasure map sailing the ocean blue in search of a hidden treasure. The pirate knows the treasure is out there. The map says so and the location of it is marked with a cross (or 'X'). All he has to do is follow the map and go to it.

But unlike the pirates we read about or hear in the movies, this pirate doesn't dig up the treasure and load it on his ship and take it back home with him. He hides it again and returns home to sell everything he owns. He later returns and buys the land where he found it. This tells me that not only does the treasure have great value, but the location has a great value, too. And by finding it, it brought the pirate joy. This must have been an awesome find.

This is very symbolic of being a Christian. Before we were saved, we were lost and searching for a better life. One day we heard about Jesus and His treasure map, the Bible, and we followed it to receive the treasure, His salvation. It was marked with the 'cross' - the cross at Calvary.

This treasure is so awesome that we didn't want to hoard it all to ourselves. Actually, we realized how great it was and how insignificant our previous life was that we chose to invest in it. Just like the man from the parable that bought the field. His intent was to build a new life on it. This included a life for him, his family, his friends, and possibly anyone that he came in contact with.

Salvation is a treasure and it comes from Jesus. It's a gift from Heaven and it brings life eternally. Are you searching for treasure today? You won't find it in money and material things. These things can fade away. The greatest treasure you will ever find is a relationship with Jesus Christ and His gift of eternal life.

For where your treasure is, there will your heart be also. - Luke 12:34

Examine your heart today. You are holding the map that's marked with the cross. What you do with it is up to you.

The Pearls
Matthew 13:45, 46

Do you know a great deal when you see it? Let's pretend for a moment that you were a jeweler. You make a living from finding precious jewels and reselling them. Because you are in the business, you have seen it all. You have made some good investments and even some bad ones. You know which ones work for your business and the ones that don't. Your experience has given you a lot of knowledge in this area.

One day in your business adventures, you stumble across a fine pearl. Pearls are a fast seller in your business, but this one is special. It's unique and you know it's very valuable. You are willing to sell everything you own in order to get it. Nothing compares to the value of this pearl that you found, so you buy it.

This is what the kingdom of Heaven is like according to this parable. Jesus is telling us how precious and valuable it is.

We all live in this world and we have experienced some of the things it has to offer. We have seen some beautiful places, heard many beautiful sounds, and tasted of some great foods. For many of us, we have experienced things in life that we thought were good, but turned out to be bad in the end. But, the one thing we all have in common is that we are searching for life's jewels. We are 'life' jewelers trying to find 'pearls' (pleasures) in this life.

I don't know about you, but I haven't found anything that lasted. I have taken vacation trips that were fun while I was there, but reality hit and I had to come back home and be left with the memory. I consider my family a pearl, but the sad thing is that they will not always be with me. I have even eaten some great tasting food, but we all know where it ends up.

The point is that there is nothing here that lasts. Being saved and living for the Lord is my 'pearl of great value'. I am promised eternal life in Jesus. My hope is in Him and my faith is strengthened while I am here because of the things He has done and is doing in my life. I am investing in my future. How about you?

The Fishing Net
Matthew 13:47-50

The kingdom of Heaven is described as a fishing net, the world is the sea, and we are all the fish. Try and picture that in your mind for a moment.

There will come a day when the Great Fisherman will drop His net into the sea and scoop up all the fish and pull it ashore. At this point, the sorting begins. The good ones will go into the basket and the bad ones will be thrown away. This will be a terrible day for a bad fish. Won't it? I guess the question right now is what type of fish we are.

If you are saved, you are a good fish. It's not because you have a fish sticker emblem on the side your car window. It's because you prayed to Jesus and asked for forgiveness of your sins and for Him to come into your life and save you. It's not because you are a good person, but because you are good by the grace of the One that saved you.

If you have never asked Jesus into your heart, you are basically...a bad fish. There's no other way to say it. But, it's not too late! If you are reading this and feel the Lord is talking to you, you have a choice to make. What are you going to do about it?

We do not know when the Lord is coming back, but we know He is. The time is closer than we think and we are getting closer to it every day. Are you prepared to meet Him? If not, I would take that step today. Ask Him to come into your life and save you.

The Workers in the Harvest
Matthew 20: 1-16

In case you didn't catch it from the parable, we, as born again Christians are workers for the Lord. If you're not doing anything, you are either waiting for your assignment or you're just flat out lazy. Regardless, we are still workers for the Kingdom of God.

The cool thing for me from this is that everyone is the same and none is greater than the other. So many times we look at what other Christians are doing for the Lord and we compare it to what we are doing. We will either get jealous or become envious or we will get filled with pride in our own efforts. I hate to be the one to bust your bubble, but God sees it all as the same. He just wants us to be working.

Are you sitting idle today? Are there things you know you should be doing for the Lord? What are you waiting on? Get up! Get out there! And get going!

How about you? You got an awesome ministry, don't you? Great things are really happening around you and you are blessed. It makes you wonder about the little guys though. Their little 'rinky dink' ministry needs to step up and become like yours. Right? I mean look at all the great things you are doing. STOP!! Maybe it would be a great idea for you to help them. It's just a thought.

And what about you? Yes, your ministry is small and you may think it's insignificant. But, God put you in it, didn't He? Just maybe He has a different purpose for your ministry and doesn't want you to be like the others. If that's the case, you may not want to strive to be like them. Just use what He has given you and move forward.

Ministry isn't about competing - it's about winning lost souls for Jesus. Take your eyes off of everybody else and put your focus on the Lord. He's the One in charge - not YOU! In His eyes, we are all equal - no one is greater!

He just wants us to be moving and to obedient to His call. And out of obedience, we should do His will - not ours.

The Growing Wheat
Mark 4: 26-29

This parable explains how ministering and spreading the Gospel works. If you are a Christian, you have a commission, given by Jesus, to tell others the Good News (the Gospel).

And Jesus came and spake unto them, saying, All power is given unto me in heaven and in earth. Go ye therefore, and teach all nations, baptizing them in the name of the Father, and of the Son, and of the Holy Ghost: Teaching them to observe all things whatsoever I have commanded you: and, lo, I

am with you alway, even unto the end of the world. Amen.Matthew 28: 18-20

Here's the problem. For one, many of us don't take the commission seriously or we think that it doesn't apply to us. We will both sit down and do nothing or we will avoid talking to people about Jesus. If we think about it, it seems useless. Doesn't it? I mean, what could we possibly say to someone that could possibly make them change their ways and begin a relationship with Jesus? If you look at the people that actually try to spread the Gospel, it appears that they are just wasting their time. Nobody cares about what they have to say. Right? Their words go in one in ear and out the other.

A good example would be this ministry that I am in. People spend their valuable time writing blogs, posting bulletins, drawing silly cartoons, creating music, and other things. For what? Nobody reads it! Nobody listens to the music or cares about cartoons! So, what's the point? Sounds like someone has too much time on their hands. They should do something more constructive!

Here's the deal and it's a mystery! As Christians with a commission, we are sharing God's Word to others. His Word has power in itself! People try to beef it up and make it 'catchy' or 'sellable', but you don't have to. The Word does its own thing. All we have to do is put it out there to people we meet and come in contact with. The parable above tells us the process.

Remember, the Lord is ultimately in control of everything. He puts people and life's events in motion. He will create situations for people to share His Word. All we have to do is be obedient and do it. Many can testify to this fact. When you surrender to the Lord and say 'use me', you will be placed in situations where someone needs to hear God's Word...from YOU!! And that little bit you share with them will manifest itself in that person and will start growing. They may not accept salvation right there on the spot, but you have planted a seed. The Lord may move them to someone else and the process is repeated. Your efforts will not be in vain!

For as the rain cometh down, and the snow from heaven, and returneth not thither, but watereth the earth, and maketh it bring forth and bud, that it may give seed to the sower, and bread to the eater: So shall my word be that goeth forth out of my mouth: it shall not return unto me void, but it shall accomplish that which I please, and it shall prosper in the thing whereto I sent it. - Isaiah 55:10, 11

How many lost people have you came in contact with? Last month? Last week? Today? These were your opportunities. Did you miss it?

It's not about what we think when it comes to our work for the Lord! That's up to Him!

Trust in the LORD with all thine heart; and lean not unto thine own understanding.- Proverbs 3:5

Out of obedience to the Lord, plant seeds. Don't think about how it all works! Time is a gift God has given you and if you are using it for Him, it is not wasted! Look for the opportunities!

The Loaned Money
Matthew 25: 14-30

This is a parable about service. Serving the Lord! But how? I am saved and ready to work! What can I do?

Let me turn my hat around and 'bust out' with a question:

Whatchu workin' with?

The Lord has given us all the tools we will need to serve Him. Some of us have had them since the day we were born! Many of us are still developing them, but what we have is useable. I believe the purpose of this parable is let you know that you have the 'tools for the trade' and that you need to use them for the Lord. So, what tools do you have?

These can be your talents. What special gift or gifts do you have? Is it singing? Writing? A lot of stuff could fall in this category and everybody's gift will be different. These talents were given to you by God to be used for His glory. It's probably something you developed at a young age. Take a close look at your talents and pray for guidance on how to use them.

These can be your abilities. Are you a good speaker? Teacher? If the Lord has gifted you with ability, it will be one that you are passionate about it. You will enjoy doing it. He has given you this for you to use for Him. There's probably an 'opening' for you at your local church. Plug in.

This could be your time. Do you have a lot of time on your hands? We waste a lot of hours out of any given day. Did you know your 'free' time was given to you by God? What are you doing with it? Are you reading His Word? Ministering to the needs of others? This could be helping others in their ministry or helping in community efforts. The Lord will open doors of opportunity for you to use the time He has given you.

It could also be your money. Are you loaded with a cash flow? It could be that the Lord wants you to share it by helping others. There are a lot of people in need. But be careful! You are also to be a good steward with it, too. This means watching out for 'moochers'.

Being a Christian that's living for Jesus opens us up to give to everyone. It doesn't matter who they are as long as their hands are out. People like to take advantage of people like that and will if you're not careful. This includes people that don't try to help themselves and even churches. But don't let this discourage you from giving! Pray for wisdom on how the Lord wants you to use what He has given you.

Just understand that God has given these things to you according to His purpose - whatever it is! He knows what He wants you to do with it. Just ask Him. The worst thing we can do is bury what we are suppose to be 'working with'. If we don't use it, it defeats the purpose for which it was intended: for the glory of God!! You hear me?

Let's make an investment today! Let's invest in the kingdom with all that we have and all that we are! It all belongs to the Lord anyway! Right?

The Nobleman's Servant
Luke 19: 11-27

Long before Jesus walked the Earth, it was prophesied that a king would come and save Israel. They expected someone great in appearance and stature. Instead, they received Jesus. Yes, He met the criteria, but He lacked the appearance of what they expected. They didn't want to believe that this man was the one they had been waiting for. However, some did.

Those of us that follow Jesus know Him as our King and Lord and Savior. We are His servants. We know that He rules over all - the saved and the lost. The lost may not realize that He rules over them - but He does and they are His subjects. The sad thing is that they are not for Him, but against Him.

To us, as servants, He has entrusted us with a responsibility - to spread His Word to the world. Each of us has been given gifts and talents according to our abilities. He doesn't give us more than what we can handle and will not give us something that He will not prepare us to do. I believe there are many in 'positions' that should not be there. The Lord did not put them in it, but may have intended for them to be doing something else. You have to look at what He has been training us to do - the gifts and talents. Since the day

199

we were born, we were being groomed and trained for His mighty work. What are yours?

Now, here's the next question. Are you using what he has given you for His glory and for His purpose? There are many churches today that have people sitting in the pews that could be doing something in the church. Just in the church that I attend, I see many singers, musicians, speakers, and teachers that are sitting down and not being active. They could be filling some positions within the church to help it grow and reach out to the lost. They could be ministering to others with what the Lord has entrusted them with. If you don't use it, you could lose it!

I believe the parable mentioned above is a lesson on ministry work and what God expects from us. It is also a lesson on making investments for the Kingdom of Heaven. He has given us all something to contribute. He is leaving it up to us to decide if we want to invest it or not and we will all be judged accordingly. This is some serious stuff!

Don't be like the servant that sat on what He was given. Put it to work and watch it draw interest for the Lord. Don't let fear hold you down. Let's get moving!

If you're not sure of what you are supposed to contribute, take a look at what you know. What are your skills, talents, and abilities? Make a list and ask the Lord to open doors of opportunities and let Him know that… you are reporting for duty!

The Servant's Role

Luke 17: 7-10

Ouch! This parable is a reminder to me and possibly to many of you reading this as to what our roles are as Christians; servants to the Lord. We should apply it as a 'wake up call' and take our roles seriously.

Even earlier in my Christian walk, I always knew God loved me and looked after me. I could see Him looking down from Heaven above watching my life. I knew that when I prayed, He listened and would answer me in His timing. It was like being saved gave me this 'magic lamp' and when I needed something in my life, I could rub the lamp and pray, and it would be given to me. This is only part of the relationship because thinking this way is only one-sided. It's all about me! Don't get me wrong. The Lord will provide for you and will hear and answer your prayers, but He does expect things from us, too. I didn't know that before.

Let me get this point across real quick. We don't earn or work for our Salvation. It is a free gift that Jesus gives and has already paid for at the cross at Calvary. He did this for you! There is nothing you have to do, except realize that you are a lost sinner needing a Savior. The Holy Spirit will convict your heart and one day you will 'wake up' and know you need Jesus in your life. At this point, you pray to Him asking for forgiveness of your sins and ask Him to come into your life and He will save you. It's a done deal!

However, as a child of God saved by His grace, you are also His servant. You have responsibilities to Him to help grow the Kingdom of God. Many of us may have a problem with this because we don't want to be tied down. Our 'rebellious youth' mindset starts kicking in because we really don't want to know that we have any obligations or duties to our Father in Heaven. But, we do. We are His servants!

Now, many of us are past this point and are OK with serving the Lord. We know what we are supposed to do and we do it. But, we do it and expect something in return - a reward for our efforts. If you think about it, we work our worldly jobs and expect our paychecks. Right? Many times we do a service for someone and they either repay the favor or 'cut us a check'. Are you with me? Our service for the Lord is different.

We are told what to do from His Word and by what He lays on our hearts. We should make every effort to accomplish the goals and assignments He has given us. Don't do it for a 'pat on the back' or for money and don't expect anything in return. Do it because of your love for the Master. Jesus came to this world as an example to us; to learn from Him and do as He did. He came as a servant folks! We should, too!

Man, this is good stuff! Put aside pride and anything that prevents us from doing what the Lord has us to do. We have a responsibility! Let's make sure we are serving and living up to our requirements. It's your duty!

The Friend at Midnight
Luke 11:5-8

There's a few things going on here and it's pretty interesting.

In case you don't know, this is a parable about prayer. It's about how the Lord expects us to be when we bring our problems and cares to Him. It's also about friendship.

In our prayers, the key word here is 'bold'. As children of God, we are to be bold when we seek Him in prayer. I looked up the word in the dictionary, out of curiosity, and it gave me some additional words that have the same meaning: fearless and confident. These are attitudes, and according to the parable, is what causes the friend to react to his friend's needs. This is the attitude the Lord wants from us for Him to move in our situations and problems. Don't confuse this attitude with being rude, arrogant, and demanding. This is different.

The Lord also wants us to come to Him knowing that He loves us and that He wants to answer our prayers. He wants a friendship relationship with us. What is our attitude when we come to the Lord? And how do we see Jesus when we pray? Do you see Him as a friend?

Think about your closest friend for a moment...your BFF (best friend forever). You can go to them with anything. You can ask them for favors and know that they will help in any way they can. Right? You can be bold, fearless, and confident. Your BFF will be there for you anytime and anywhere. You know this because you trust them. They are your BFF.

On the flip side, if you're like me, you may not be good at the whole friendship making process and may not ask anybody for anything. This is a prideful attitude and will affect your prayers. We may not ask the Lord for anything and rely on ourselves and our own strength. This is a wall that needs to be torn down in our lives! If we can see Jesus as a friend, our prayers will get answered and things will start happening in our life and in the lives of the people that we pray for. Jesus wants to be your BFF.

On another note based on the parable, if one of our friends came to us with a problem, we would try our best to help them. Right? If they came at midnight, I'm sure we would try to help them the next day unless they were persistent. Not because they were bugging us to death but because we would know that they seriously needed some help right then...right now. We would wake up and help them.

Knowing that, we need to express the seriousness of our needs to the Lord in prayer. I wouldn't throw a few half-hearted words up in the air. If someone has asked you to pray for them, pray with sincerity. Your friend needs your help - your prayers. Do you really want to help them? Express your sincerity to the Lord. Let Him know you are serious. Be bold about it!

According to the parable, we have an example of friendship relationships. It's like a friend is helping a friend help a friend. Do you see it? You are the one in the middle; an intercessor for someone in need. They are a friend of yours asking you for help. At the moment, you can't help them, but instead of pushing them aside, you seek help from a friend you know. You go to him on their behalf. You could have just told them your friend's name and sent them over to his house to ask for help, taking you completely out of the loop. But the point is, they came to you first and probably don't know your friend. Would you ask for help from someone you don't know? What if a friend referred you? Probably not. But when they receive the help they need through your 'connection', they may decide to go to him directly the next time they are in need. This is where your prayers become a ministry tool in leading someone to the Lord. Now it gets serious!

Just know that as a Christian, you have a friend in Jesus. When you pray, you are praying to your BFF; your Best Friend Forever. Forever is a long time - it's eternal. Tear down those walls that prevent you from having this friendship relationship with our Savior. When you see Him as a friend, new doors will begin opening up and your walk will become better.

If people come into your life needing prayer, don't think of it as another name to the prayer list. Think of it as an opportunity from God to you! You are now the link to either their new relationship or their link to a stronger relationship with the Lord. Be glad! The Lord is using you!

204

The Unjust Judge
Luke 18: 1-8

The big word from this parable is 'persistence'. Praying without giving up! That's not the only thing I received from this parable. It reveals the character of the One we pray to - God. He is a just God and He delivers. He delivers because He loves us and cares about us.

Jesus used the illustration to show the difference between the God we serve and a judge that doesn't care about people or doesn't fear the Lord. The judge answered the widow's request, but it was only after she bugged him to death. He was more concerned with himself than the widow in need. God's not like that!

We serve a God that cares! When we pray to Him, He listens. He may not answer our prayers right away. It could be that He is waiting for the proper time to deliver. This is called 'answering our prayers in His timing - not ours'. I'm sure you have heard of this or have experienced this in your life. To answer a prayer, the moment has to be perfect. This may involve preparing our hearts to receive it. A lot of things can happen to us spiritually during this time of 'waiting'.

We can give up!
This is where you stop praying for it to happen and decide to give up on God and pursue answering your prayer yourself. Spiritually, this is turning your back on God. Faith destroyed!

We can keep on praying!
This is where you continue to 'plead your case'. This builds our character by acknowledging our helplessness and need for God in our lives. This is a humbling experience. Being humble is where God wants us to be! This takes self out of the picture. We continue to seek Him and we put our faith in action.

Being persistent develops faith and faith develops perseverance. There is an awesome scripture on this topic:

Knowing this, that the trying of your faith worketh patience. But let patience have her perfect work, that ye may be perfect and entire, wanting nothing. If any of you lack wisdom, let him ask of God, that giveth to all men liberally, and upbraideth not; and it shall be given him. But let him ask in faith, nothing wavering. For he that wavereth is like a wave of the sea driven with the wind and tossed. For let not that man think that he shall receive any thing of the Lord.
- James 1: 3-7

Are you praying for something today? Are you waiting for your prayer to be answered? It could be that the Lord is preparing you for it. Have you totally surrendered yourself to Him? He is looking for faithful servants. Will you be one of them?

Allow Him to grow you as a Christian. Put your faith in action and believe that He will answer your prayer. Be persistent in your request to Him and never give up! Never give up!

The Good Samaritan
Luke 10: 30-37

In this parable, Jesus is replying to a question given by an expert of the law on how to inherit eternal life. Being an expert in the law, you would think he would know the answer. Jesus reversed the question and asked him what the law says and what it meant to him. By doing so, this made the man repeat it to himself.

The man said, "Love the Lord your God with all your heart and with all your soul and with all your strength and with all your mind'; and, 'Love your neighbor as yourself.'"

But, the man seemed to have a problem with the last part, so he asked Jesus, "Who is my neighbor?" At this question, Jesus gave this parable and was His answer.

A person can be very knowledgeable of the Bible and still be spiritually dumb. You can have the ability to recite the Bible word for word and front to back, but if you don't apply it to your life, it won't mean 'a hill of beans' to you. You have to be open spiritually and allow the Holy Spirit to reveal to you what its saying. The Bible isn't a best-selling novel because the stories are good. It's because it's spiritual food for our soul!

I remember as a child having to learn and recite Psalms 23. I kept reading it over and over until I was able to repeat it. To me, it was just a bunch of words, but I learned it. I didn't know what it meant. It was several years later when I was actually in a dark time in my life when that scripture hit home. It became a promise to me that the Lord was with me. I was able to hold onto it and it got me through.

According to the parable, this expert of the law had some issues. He knew the law front to back, but had difficulty with loving others. Love is the key factor in our walk with the Lord. The Bible says God is love and that He loves us. Not only are we to love Him, but we are also to love others. God even gave us an example of His love towards us that He sent His Son to die for us.

In His parable, a man was robbed, beaten and left to die on the side of the road. Jesus used examples of various people that walked by this man and each one had an opportunity to help. First, there was a priest. You would think he would help. I'm sure with his title, he has helped people many times, but he didn't. Second, there was the Levite. Levites were workers in the Temple. They were known for singing, building, teaching, ministering, and I'm sure there were many jobs they did for the Temple. Did the Levite help? Nope. It was when the Samaritan passed by that the man was helped.

An important thing to know here is that Jesus was speaking to a Jewish community. The Jews hated the Samaritans. Why would Jesus use a parable that showed a Samaritan as the good guy to a crowd of Jews? It would have been a slap in the face.

I believe the answer is simple and applies to a lot of Christians today. When the Bible says 'love thy neighbor', it's not just talking about our fellow brothers and sisters in Christ. It's not just talking about our families and friends. A neighbor is more than the people living next door. It's wide open! It means everybody – worldwide!

We can't segregate people and decide to love only the ones we choose. We can't put the good ones on the right and the bad ones on the left and give our attention to the good ones. When we do, our backs are turned toward the bad ones. Who are we to decide who is good or bad anyway? We are all neighbors on this big planet!

We are told to love everybody. How do we show love? It is through mercy; the same mercy that Jesus showed us. When we do, it will break the walls of racism, walls of pride, walls of anger and hate...let the walls fall!!

When opportunities come knocking in your life for you to show 'good', be the one to open the door.

The Wedding Feast

Luke 14: 7-11

There was a dinner party going on at a well known Pharisees house. I'm sure many people were invited and it was a big event. Jesus got an invitation, too.

As the guests arrived and were picking out their places to sit, Jesus watched them. My vision is a large room with many tables. The more elegant tables were possibly placed near the front of the excitement. The people that sat there may have received special treatment or would be recognized as special people. I can only assume that this was an 'open' banquet and people could sit wherever they wanted, but the best seats in the house were these. Who wouldn't want to sit there? Right?

Jesus noticed this and told His parable. When you first read it, you automatically think this is a parable of how we, as Christians, are to be humble and stay in the shadows or in 'low' positions and wait for someone to move us up. It is, but I feel there is more to it than just that. I believe Jesus saw something 'ugly' that day. He saw pride and how it affects people.

Every one of us has had some form of pride in our life and for some it can be a battle at times. It's not a gift from God, but a worldly attitude. A harmful side of pride is when we try to attract everyone's attention on us. We may not mean to, but it happens. The result is that people will recognize this pride in a person and will quickly turn away from them. If you're in a ministry trying to lead others to Christ and it begins drawing attention to who you are instead of the One you are serving, people will stop listening to you. Your ministry will lose the effectiveness it was intended.

Another form of pride is when you belittle yourself and the abilities that God has given you. An example would be if you had a singing voice and you refuse to use it because of what you think of yourself. We think we are being humble by not stepping forward, but the reality is that we are thinking of ourselves. This is a form of pride, too. The negative side to this is that the people your gift from God was supposed to reach will not benefit from it. What if this person was lost? God may have given you this talent solely for that one moment of service for Him.

I believe another lesson from this parable is of protection. Jesus wanted to protect us from what happens when our pride gets busted. This is a feeling of discouragement. Discouragement is a powerful weapon from Satan. If he can make you feel discouraged, he will have you tied down. It is paralyzing to the point to where you don't want to move or do anything. It's a depressed feeling that makes you want to sit down.

In ministry, we should focus that 'thing' we do towards Jesus. Remember, we are doing it for Him. We are His vessels. He, in turn, will use us and direct us in it. When we know that He is in control of it, we shouldn't get discouraged because its all in His hands - not ours. If things don't happen the way we think they should or your ministry isn't advancing like it should,...oh well. Jesus is still in control. The key here is to not focus on 'self' at all. Let the Lord do it.

The parable could also reflect how we should do our ministry work. Humble ourselves in it. Be willing to take the lowest places. When the host, Jesus, is ready to place us at an honorable table, He will. It's all up to Him and His timing. Just use what you got and where He has placed you and take 'self' completely out of it.

The Proud Pharisee and the Corrupt Tax Collector

Luke 18: 9-14

Here we have some examples of people and the message seems to be directed towards religious people and the lost and how they present themselves to the Lord. Here we have two men praying. One is a Pharisee and the other is a tax collector. We know from the Bible that a Pharisee was a 'religious' person and looked good in the eyes of the people around them. A tax collector wouldn't get that same response.

The problem in the Pharisee's prayer was that he was boasting about himself and his accomplishments for the Lord. To put it in today's language, it would be like 'Look at me Lord. Look at what I'm doing!' And the other issue is how he compared himself with others. He was putting them down to make himself look better. It was almost as if he thought his works justified him.

It mentions that there is a penalty for people acting like this. It says that a person that exalts himself will be humbled. I'm sure you can think of many ways a proud person can be brought down a few steps. Personally, I wouldn't want to be in their shoes. But, God has a way of putting us in our place.

The tax collector, however, knew his position with the Lord. He was a sinner and he knew it. He was very humble and asked for God's mercy. He must have known all the wrong that he had done and asked for forgiveness. Because of this he was justified.

Justified is the key word in this parable. Justification is God's act of declaring or making a sinner righteous before Himself. We are justified by faith in Jesus and His death on the cross. This cannot be accomplished by our good deeds or our works for Him. We are justified when we ask the Lord to forgive us of our sins and turn from them and by asking Jesus to come into our lives and save us. God will forgive us and justify us. There is a message in this for us and it's very important.

If you have never asked Jesus to come into your life and asked for His forgiveness of all the junk you have done, you are lost. It doesn't matter if you are a member of a church. It doesn't matter if you are doing great things in your community. You are lost and you need a Savior. There are so many people today calling themselves Christians because they consider themselves 'good' people or because of their status in the church.

The fact is, if you have never humbled yourself in prayer to Jesus Christ and called out to Him, you are missing the important part. Are you saved? If not, get it squared up. There are no magic words to repeat - it's a prayer between you and God. Ask Him for forgiveness of your sins, turn from the junk you do, believe that He died on the cross for you and rose again, and then accept Him into your life. That's it! Only God can justify you. It's your call!

The Rich Fool
Luke 12: 16-21

Before I begin writing about this parable, I would like to mention the verses before and after it:

And he said unto them, Take heed, and beware of covetousness: for a man's life consisteth not in the abundance of the things which he possesseth.- Luke 12: 15

And he said unto his disciples, Therefore I say unto you, Take no thought for your life, what ye shall eat; neither for the body, what ye shall put on. - Luke 12: 22

Today, as I write this, our world is in a big financial mess. There are a lot of money issues going on; banks are going bankrupt, people are losing their jobs and their homes, and the world is in a big turmoil. What caused all of this? If I could narrow it all down to a single word, I would say 'greed'. Everyone is trying to store up 'bigger barns'. The banks create loans with the hopes of people not being able to pay them back and thus, receiving the assets at a fraction of the original cost. And

people borrowing money for things beyond their means that they know that they can't pay back. What happens in the end? No one gets anything!

In the parable, Jesus gives us an example of someone that wanted an over abundance of 'stuff'. The problem for him is that he didn't have a place for it, so he had to build bigger storage. And when he accumulated as much 'stuff' as he wanted, he thought he could just kick back and relax, but God told him that his life would be taken that very night. So, knowing that, who would get his 'stuff'? It definitely wouldn't be him. So all of that saving and storing would be in vain and would be handed down to someone else. The sad thing is that he never got a chance to enjoy living. He spent all of his time saving and building storage barns.

Jesus tells His disciples (and us as Christians) to guard themselves (ourselves) against greed. Living isn't about building up your possessions. Actually He tells us not to worry about our life and material things. Our focus should be totally on Him. He is our Provider. Our 'stuff' is given to us by Him. Did you know that?

People work so hard every day and work multiple jobs to gain material items. Many of them don't have time to enjoy them. It's sad, but we have become a materialistic world. What would it take to get everyone back on track?

Maybe a recession. Maybe it would take losing the things we couldn't really afford anyway and replacing it with something affordable and reasonable. Maybe it would take losing a job that we work too hard at anyway; that was probably killing us with all of its stress. Maybe being home will help us realize that we have a family. Maybe... just maybe we will realize that we need God in our life and that we need Him to provide for our needs because we can't do it on our own. Just maybe.

The Great Feast

Luke 14:16-24

Excuses - everyone has one. If you want to hear some good ones, ask your kids why they haven't completed their homework or cleaned their room. All sorts of reasons spring forth and some are kinda' funny.

Jesus is giving us an example of a man giving a banquet. For a simple man like me, this would be similar to someone preparing a huge dinner table laid out with all the best Southern cooking you could possibly ask for. I picture fried chicken, fresh black-eyed peas, and possibly cornbread or homemade biscuits. And then over to the side somewhere, there is the banana pudding. Yummy! Sounds good doesn't it?

The invitations had been sent out, but nobody has shown up. So the man sends his servants out to find out why they are running late. Then, here come the excuses:

"I bought some land and I want to look at it."

I'm sure the land isn't going anywhere. Look at it later and go eat!

"I bought five oxen and I want to try them out."

The oxen can take care of themselves and working can wait until after dinner!

"I got married, so I can't come."

EXCUSES... EVERYBODY HAS ONE!

Take your spouse with you! They got to eat, too!

These are excuses, but they are not good enough reasons to turn down free food. When my wife tells me dinner is ready, I have no problem in stopping what I'm doing. Do you?

I think we already know that this parable symbolizes accepting Jesus as Lord and Savior into our lives. We all have an invitation, but we quickly give our excuses for not wanting to take part. We say our life is too busy for a relationship with Him. We use the excuses of work, activities, and the influences of others to keep us from Him, but personally, there are no real excuses. It's free - and it doesn't cost you a dime.

After seeing how bad the world had become, God could have destroyed it long ago and started all over. But He loves us and sent His Son to prepare us the way to receive the 'banquet'. We need to put aside our excuses and just go -

accept Him into your life. What's your excuse? You have the invitation!

The Shrewd Manager
Luke 16: 1-9

Most commentaries you read on this parable tell us that we should use our worldly possessions for the good of others. They are given to us by God to help people. In the process, we make friends and God will bless us. By giving, we develop a Christ-like behavior and it will help us grow spiritually. This is the main point of this parable.

The manager mentioned in this parable had some issues. He wasted the possessions that were entrusted to him by the rich man that he worked for. After reading the whole parable, it appears that he did this by 'gouging' his debtors - overcharging them. By wasting his possessions, he could have made it impossible for the debtors to pay it back. I can only assume this because the rich man commended him when he settled the debts at a much lower payback. Plus, it says that he was dishonest. The manager may have been prideful and felt that he could charge people anything he wanted - simply because he could. His 'boss' or 'master' was the money. By doing this, people may have hated him.

The rich man had a problem with this behavior and decided to do away with the manager's job. What was this manager going to do now? He was too weak to work and felt bad to ask people for help because of the wrong that he had done to them. So, the manager came up with a clever plan. He made things right with the debtors. In the process, he made friends. Being shrewd is characterized by making smart decisions. The manager returned the borrowed merchandise back to the rich man while making friends with the debtors. At this point, he focused on his job and what his 'boss' had wanted him to do.

The parable ends with a comparison between people of this world and the people of the light. The difference in the two is in the master that they serve: God or Money.

The world uses money as a power tool. As Christians, we are given material possessions to use for the glory of God and to help others. When we help someone, we show God's love and mercy through our actions. But, for some of us, we take the worldly approach and use what He has given us for our own pleasure or for gaining more wealth. We should also treat all people fairly in our dealings in money matters and not take advantage of them. This is another Christ-like behavior.

If we can ever get to the point that we realize that God is in control of everything - money included - and know that it is He that gave it to us to use for Him, we will know that we are to be managers of it. He can give us more. Money becomes a witnessing tool to reach others for Jesus. It's kind of like giving a Bible tract that people will actually read. It could give you a chance to give a person your testimony and they could possibly get saved. Money talks people listen.

Instead of debating on whether you should help someone, just do it. Don't judge them. If you got it, give it. If God gave you money to spend - use it to witness to a friend.

The Lost Sheep
Luke 15: 3-7

We read this parable and realize the love that Jesus has for us. If you have never accepted Jesus as Savior, He loves you, too. When someone comes to the Lord and repents of their sins, all of Heaven rejoices - it's a celebration. We should follow His example.

I believe this parable is talking to anyone involved in ministry and it's talking to the church. We have a purpose and it's not just satisfying the needs of its members and its current congregation. There's a world outside your window and there are people out there that are lost - just like the lost sheep mentioned in the scripture.

If you're a church, what are you doing to bring them in? So many times we sit and wait for them to show up for services. The sad thing is that they may not come unless they are invited. We can't be content with just the '99 in the open country'. Chances are, these folks are already saved. What about the 'one'? You know the one that you ignored at the grocery store or that you work with on a daily basis. What about them? Do they need Jesus? If so, invite them to church - bring them home.

And the lord said unto the servant, Go out into the highways and hedges, and compel them to come in, that my house may be filled. - Luke 14:23

The same applies to ministries. Where are you ministering at? Is it to a saved congregation? Depending on your ministry, there are opportunities outside the four walls you are currently working in. The lost are LOST and may not know how to find their way. Take your ministry to them. Ask the Lord to show you how to make your ministry more effective for His glory. The doors will start opening.

One of the things about finding a 'lost sheep', is that you have to 'physically' look for it. This involves moving. The chance of a 'lost sheep' wandering to where you are is slim to none. Go find it and bring it home.

Do you want to rejoice? Help a lost sheep find Jesus. You will be telling everybody and having a 'Hallelujah fit' and celebrating. It's an awesome feeling! Go get 'em!!

The Lost Coin
Luke 15: 8-10

In this parable, Jesus uses lost money (silver coins) to describe how precious one lost sinner is. My Bible mentions that the Palestinian women in those days received ten silver coins as a wedding gift. So, besides having a monetary value, these coins had a sentimental value like that of a wedding ring and to lose one would be a bad thing.

After losing the coin, the woman from the parable goes on an extensive search for it. I mean she lights a lamp and sweeps the whole house. I bet she searched every crack and corner and even in the dark areas. This coin means something to her - it's precious!

Try to imagine losing something of yours that has special value to you. To what extreme would you go to in order to find it? This is how we should be to the lost people in this world. I believe many dried up churches would have their joy restored if they shared the same love and concern for the lost that Jesus has. We should take the Gospel with us and share it with everyone we meet and not leave it behind the four walls of a worship building.

It could almost be like losing your child at the local Wally World. If

this happened to you, what would you do? Leave them there and expect them to just 'be OK' by themselves? No way! Our kids are special to us and we would search high and low until they were found. Am I right? God feels the same way about us and expects us to go on a 'child' hunt. Know what I'm saying?

We need to reach out to the lost, folks! We can't just sit still and wait for them to come to us. We need to let our light shine in this world and search everywhere until we find them. Invite them to church and tell them about Jesus. Jesus loves them and so should we!

The Lost Son
Luke 15: 11-32

This is a lot of reading, but it is very important and it's good stuff. This describes the love God has for us. No matter how far away we are from Him - lost or out of His will - He still loves us and wants us to come home.

God sent His Son to die on a cross for the sins of the world - our sins. He has offered to us a gift of Salvation - it's our choice to accept it. To receive it, all we have to do is turn from our sins and ask for forgiveness and accept Jesus into our life. Jesus is the greatest gift of all!

There are many people who are saved, but choose to follow the ways of the world. This path leads to destruction. They are lost, not because they lost their salvation, but because they have strayed away from their Father in Heaven.

As brothers and sisters in Christ, we should encourage one another. If we know someone that has drifted away, we should reach out and help them. Satan is tricky and wants to hurt God's children. We should work together.

If you're saved today, but you're not living like it, it's time to come back home. Don't reach rock bottom before you realize that you have made a big mistake. Call out to Him and turn around. Jesus is waiting and He's waiting for you.

The Forgiven Debts
Luke 7: 41-43

Reading this parable made me think, "How is love measured?" In my own little world, I say 'I love you' all the time. I say 'I love you' every day to my wife and kids and it has become a habit before bed time. I may tell them occasionally throughout the day. On the days that I call my mother on the phone, I make it a point to tell her, too. All of these people play a big part in my life. I love them all very much.

I also love my other family members and my friends, but not as much as the ones that are close to me. I am just being honest and many of you will agree with me. As a Christian, I even love people that I just met. But this kind of love ranks at the bottom of the list. I love them, but it doesn't compare to the love I have for my family. Knowing this, I realize that love can be measured.

Then, I ask myself, "Do I love Jesus?" I have never met Him personally. Before I was saved, I heard about Him from church, the Bible, from Christian people, and even watched a few of those Biblical Easter movies. I knew that this man died for me and my sins. At the age of 14, I became convicted in my heart and realized that I needed Him as my Savior and I asked Him to come into my life and save me. The relationship with Him began. Did I love Him? Yes, but not as much as I would

221

a family member. I think it was because I didn't know the full extent of what He did for me on the cross.

I am learning more of it now. You see, the word 'sin' is a big deal. It's part of our human nature. We do it every day. There are big ones and small ones, but they are still 'sin'. Because of it, we are separated from God - the Creator of this world. Everything you see around you is part of His creation. He intended for us to live life to the fullest, but because of sin, He has to destroy it. God is Holy. This may be hard for us to understand.

Another issue in the world is that 'sin' isn't a bad thing anymore. Everyone accepts it as part of culture and habit. People don't feel condemned over it, so they continue to do it. They also don't think there is a consequence for it either. The penalty is death, folks! Life no more! This world has made sinful acts acceptable or it's not really that big of a deal. But, if you knew your sin prevented you from eternal life, it may just wake you up.

Here's where it gets good. Jesus, the man from the Bible, was God's Son. God sent Him here as a sacrifice to make things right for everybody. He paid our sin debt when He died on the cross at Calvary. All we are required to do is to believe in Him and ask Him to forgive us of our sins. We need to turn from our sin and ask Him to come into our life. This is why it's called 'getting saved'. He is saving us from eternal death. But, by turning our lives over to Him and allowing Him to save us, He will have paid the biggest debt that we could never pay by ourselves. Our families couldn't pay that debt for us. Only Jesus.

For us that are saved, we need to realize how big of a debt He paid for us. We were doomed to die, but now we have eternal life because of Him. We should love Him more than anyone else. He should be our Number One in our life, in our home, and in the way we conduct ourselves on a daily basis.

We should follow His examples. We should read His Word and follow His instructions. Why? Because we love Him for what He has done for us. We should be thankful to Him and pray to Him always. We should remove Him from the bottom of our 'to do' list and put him at the top where He belongs. Do I love Him? Yes, I do. I love Him with all my heart, my entire mind, and all my strength. I am 'saved' because He sacrificed His life for mine. He is my hero, my Savior, and is becoming so much more every day.

There is going to be a day when our sins will be presented back to us like when we receive our bills from our creditors. This is called the Day of Judgment. If you have not accepted Jesus as Lord and Savior, Jesus will say, "I never knew you." However, for the Christian, your bill will say, "Paid in Full". Your debts have been paid. Eternal life awaits you - enter in. That's great news!

Even in a recession, Jesus is able to pay your debts. If you don't have Jesus in your life, let Him in. Do you have trouble loving Jesus the way you know you should? Pay Him a visit again at Calvary. Remember what He has done for you. No one has ever done for you what He did for you on the cross! Make things right today!

The Ten Virgins
Matthew 25: 1-13

The parable is talking about the end of times; the day Jesus returns to call His children home. He symbolizes this event with the illustration of ten virgins waiting for the bridegroom. They all know he's coming, but the problem is that they don't know when.

The same is true for us today. We have heard for years that Jesus is coming one day - the end draws near. I would imagine this has been going on for over two thousand years. Our parents have heard it. Their parents have heard it and so on and so on. But eventually over time, waiting and preparing for His return tends to get neglected and we move on to other things. I mean if He hasn't come within the past two thousand years, He may wait another two thousand years. We got plenty of time, right?

If you think about it, one of two things is going to happen in our life time. We will either die or Jesus will come back. And based on history, people have been harping on 'the end of the world' for years and nothing's happened yet. And another thing, our life expectancy is around 80 years old, so we got a lot time to do the things we want to and live how we want to. Plus, the whole

'Jesus thing' is for old folks, so we can do all that stuff around the age of fifty-something. By doing this, we can live our life to the fullest and still prepare for the day we die or Jesus' return. It sounds like a perfect plan to me. I'm glad we have figured it out. Great job! But wait…what if?

What if we face death early? I mean there is a small chance that we could be involved in a fatal accident that could take our life. I know that sounds crazy, but its worth considering. I have heard of people our age leaving this world still in their youth. That could be a problem. It's a small chance, but what if, ya' know? It could happen. It's good to plan ahead for things like this.

And what if Jesus returns earlier than we expected? The chance of this happening in our lifetime is slim to none or is it? We really don't know. The Bible says He will come like a thief in the night. We just don't want to get caught off guard like a deer in headlights. Will there be enough time to get our life together and still be prepared to meet Him?

So, what do we do? It's too much to gamble.

Wouldn't it just be easier to live for Jesus now? Are the things we want to do really that important? If, by chance, He comes tomorrow, wouldn't it be better knowing you were ready to meet Him?

Verse 13 says, *"Watch therefore, for ye know neither the day nor the hour wherein the Son of man cometh."*

We don't know when He is coming, regardless of what you read in the papers or on television. Goofy people predict the 'end time' dates all the time, but they don't know either. What it boils down to is this…watch and be ready!

When you hear the midnight cry, will you be ready? Think about it!

The Traveling Owner of the House
Mark 13: 34-37

From what I have read and understand from The Bible in the Old Testament, a porter had an important job. His duties were to simply 'watch' and keep his eyes and ears open. These porters would stand at the entrances to the tabernacles or at the entrance gates leading into the city. They would march back and forth covering the entrance area. It may seem like a simple job, but it was important.

By watching, they would be the first contact before anyone would be allowed to enter in. If it were the enemy, they could take the necessary actions to alert everyone and be prepared to defend themselves. Could you imagine what could have happened if the porter fell asleep? It wouldn't be good. The enemy could come in and destroy the city.

In the last verse of this parable, Jesus is telling all of us to 'watch'. He wants us to be like the porters from the Bible. We are to 'watch' for His coming. I believe we are also to 'watch' for the enemy that tries to invade our lives. You know who I am talking about. The Bible calls him Satan. This joker is tricky and would love to see you fall. He will put things in your life that tempt you with the hopes that you will give in to it. Whatever your weakness is will probably be what he uses against you. That's why it's important to be 'awake' and 'watch'. Read God's Word and keep yourself prayed up. It's when you decide to stop is when Satan will dance right on top of your head.

As a porter, it's important that you are moving. Just like a soldier in the army, keep marching in your ministry that God has called you to do. It's hard to fall asleep when your body is moving. Here again, when you decide to stop, you open yourself to the advances of the enemy; ol' Satan himself.

A lot of things can happen to a Christian that decides to fall asleep at the wheel in his or her walk with Christ. The chances of going in the wrong direction increases. You could easily slip, trip, and take a dip in places you don't want to be. It's best to keep our eyes on Jesus and stay awake... WATCH!!

We don't know when Jesus is returning, but it's closer than it was yesterday. Let's make sure we are doing what we are supposed to. And one more time... WATCH!!

The Wise and Faithful Servants
Luke 12: 42-48

According to the parable, there is a price to pay for disobedience. Every one of us has a job to do. If you are saved today, the Lord has given you something that you should be doing for His glory and to reach the lost. In each of us is a gift, talent, or skill that the Lord has given. Our job is to use it. So, why are so many Christian people sitting down?

We all know that our works don't save us. It is through Jesus Christ alone that we are saved. But, by being saved, we are also called to do something. It's like being hired for a job. You have abilities that God has given you. He expects you to use them and to be faithful to His call.

He is returning one day people. We don't know when, but we are guaranteed that He's coming. What will He find us doing when He returns? We can't waste away precious time when there is so much work to be done. People out there are lost and Christians are getting discouraged and everyone needs help. Your help!

You are in big demand. We need you and Jesus needs you to further His kingdom. What is your calling? Are you supposed to be preaching? Singing? Ministering to others? Praying? There are so many things I could ask and only you know what your calling is. I guess the real question should be...why aren't you doing it?

Is it pride? Are you afraid? Satan doesn't want you to do the Lord's work. He wants you to sit still. But, understand this. Greater is He that's in you than he that's in the world. Resist the devil and he will flee from you. Take a stand today and say, "I am working for the Lord beginning today and I am not letting Satan bring me down!"

If you're not sure of what you are supposed to be doing, pray and ask God to tell you. He will! And when you surrender to Him, doors of opportunity will begin opening up for you and your ministry. That's right! Ministry! Your ministry is your work for the Lord. He has one already planned just for you. Let Him know you are reporting for duty. Let's get on fire, folks!

227

The Two Sons
Matthew 21: 28-32

Jesus gave this parable in response to the religious leaders concerning His authority. These leaders were self righteous men that did good works yet did not have the heart for Jesus. Their works were out of religious obligation. They had a form of godliness like the second son from the parable, but they weren't doing the will of God.

The tax collectors and the prostitutes, after hearing the Gospel of John, had a change of heart. They didn't have a form of godliness, but after their heart changed, they began doing God's will.

This is what I feel this parable is talking about to you and I. It's all about a change of heart. In any kind of ministry, why do you do what you do? Is it because you feel you have to? Are you trying to earn 'brownie points' from God? Is it to make you look good? If you said yes, let me bust your bubble. You are doing it for the wrong reason! You have the wrong heart!

First and foremost, your 'good works' do not give you a guaranteed ticket to Eternity. Oh no! Your ticket has been blood bought by Jesus and you have to accept Him into your life. How? By asking for forgiveness of your sins

and turning from them; believing that Jesus died for you and rose again; and simply accepting Him into your heart. This is when your heart changes. When Jesus saves you, you will change. The Gospel will begin to transform your life. You won't be the same person you used to be. You will no longer want to do the old things you used to do. You won't act the way you used to act. You will want to 'work' because you are now serving the Lord. You will have a desire to reach the lost for Jesus. By doing so, you will be doing what the Father wants you to do - His will. Why? Because your heart changed.

Has your heart changed? Take the first step today by letting Jesus live in it.

The Wicked Tenants
Luke 20: 9-16

The Earth is the vineyard and God created it. He loaned it to us. It belongs to Him regardless of what our so-called 'deed papers' say. We, as human beings, are also His creation. We belong to Him, too. However, He has given us 'free will' and a freedom to choose. We can decide if we want God in our life or not. We are like the fruit of the vineyard.

According to the Old Testament, many people were persecuted for following God. God would love to see the world change, but because of 'free will', many people won't. Actually they would rather beat and send away the ones that come and try to help them see the truth. In a last resort, God sent His Son. He was nailed to the cross.

Now the time has come. God will destroy the people that have not accepted Him and will give the vineyard to others - to us that have given our lives to Him. Which one are you?

God is still sending people out into the vineyard to reach the lost. If you are reading this and don't know Jesus as your Lord and Savior, I am a messenger with Good News for you. You can be saved. Jesus loves you and wants you to have the gift of eternal life that only He offers. He died on the cross to give it to you. Yes, you have 'free will' and you have two choices:

Choice A
You can deny Him like you have done many times before.

Or, Choice B
You can say 'yes' and accept Him as your Lord and Savior. If you feel a conviction in your heart that you are lost, you need to act on it.

The Unproductive Fig Tree
Luke 13: 6-9

Being productive is when an effort produces results. It's like when a person works for a living. The result is when they receive their paycheck at the end of the week. If you're one of the few that actually enjoy their job, your result may be more than the money. It could be the product you make or maybe the smile on the person's face that you helped.

Companies try in various ways to improve productivity in their employees and the machinery they use. They offer incentive programs to award their workers if they can achieve certain numbers in finished goods or in the volume of their output. Some companies invest money into improving their machinery with hopes of it producing more. In all cases, improved productivity is a good thing.

I think one of the problems with this economic recession, is that people are being faced with a negative result to their efforts. For many of them, the years they have given working for a company has resulted in a loss of a job. I remember getting 'laid off' from a job eight years ago. This was a very sad day for me because I looked back on how long I worked there (14 years) and realized that I was just another employee. My employer didn't care!

From the parable, I believe Jesus is talking to people leading churches and to people with ministries. Jesus wants to see results. He wants you to be productive and He cares about your growth. He loves you! The man in the parable was in charge of this fig tree planted in the vineyard, but it didn't bear any fruit. It took three years and the owner saying something about it for him to stand up and start moving. He dug around it and fertilized it. I believe Jesus is the 'owner' mentioned here.

In ministry and church, we expect Jesus to do it all. In church, we think people will just walk in without us inviting them. For a church to grow, we have to fertilize it by asking folks to come. To 'bring in', you must first 'reach out'. In ministry, we need to make sure we are doing what we can, too. Dig around it and put some fertilizer on it. Watch it grow!

I also believe this parable is talking to us as Christians about our spiritual growth. If you are in the same position you were in three years ago, something is definitely wrong! You're not growing. If you're honest with yourself, you are probably not reading His Word or you have stopped going to church. And you're definitely not going to grow if you have stopped praying. You got to put some spiritual fertilizer in the mix - the Word, church, and prayer.

The ball is in your court today. You wanna grow? Then, let's grow! Grab a shovel...

The Marriage Feast
Matthew 22: 1-14

A king is having a wedding party for his son. He has sent out the invitations, but many people have refused to come. The king gets angry! And I don't blame him...

My 3 year old daughter recently had a birthday party. My wife invited as many people as she could. She called people on the telephone, sent emails, mailed invitations and told people when she would meet them in public. She wanted this to be a special occasion for our little Beth. This would be a special day.

My wife and I bought the necessary

party decorations, made the reservations at the local park, and bought the food and drinks needed and expected many people to show up. The party was ready. Then came the excuses...

Needless to say, maybe a ¼ of the people showed up that got invited. Beth still had a great birthday party, but we had a lot of leftovers to bring back home that eventually got wasted. The parable mentioned above is similar, but it's more serious than a simple birthday party. The parable above is talking about eternal life.

The Invitation
The invitations have already been sent out. Everyone is invited to receive eternal life. Jesus paid the price on the cross at Calvary. Read John 3:16. He did it for the whole world. You are included! Don't ignore it!

The Servants
Those of us that are saved should be telling the world about the Good News. The Gospel is being spread all over the place. That's what we do - what we are called to do. We gotta' get the Word out... Will you be joining us in the feast?

The Guests
These are the folks that say, "OK. Count me in!" And actually show up. These people are the ones that accept Jesus as Lord and Savior. They put on the wedding clothes and are dressed for the banquet. Some people play the game, but don't take the necessary step by asking Jesus to come into their life and repenting of their sins. You may as well not of showed up at all.

And Those That Refuse To Come
Here's the deal, according to the parable. The king is cleaning house. You are either in or you're out. And being 'out' has a very bad outcome. Look at your

invitation today. Will you be joining the feast provided by the King? I hope to see you there!

The Unforgiving Servant
Matthew 18: 23-35

This is a parable on forgiveness and mercy. I think many of us can relate to it. Even though it speaks of forgiving money debts, it also relates to forgiving and having mercy on many levels.

Forgiving and Having Mercy For Others

One thing I have learned in life is that people are human. It doesn't matter who they are. People make mistakes. The sad thing is that people's words and actions affect us. The same people that can offer us encouragement or do nice things can say or do things that can hurt us emotionally and physically.

To live in the flesh and be worldly, we will have enemies and we will have friends. To live as a Christian and be spiritual in our walk, we need to understand the importance of love. Loving our neighbor means our friends and our enemies. Satan will use these people as a tool to bring us down. He tempts them, so that through their emotions, they can lash out on us in hurtful ways. How can we survive?

First, we have to recognize the enemy. Secondly, we need to understand the many ways he will try to defeat us. Thirdly, we should apply the love to our lives that Jesus tells us about from His Word and use it as a shield. If you truly love your neighbor, then their words or actions will never hurt you. We will know who is behind it all. We will be able to forgive them and have mercy on them.

Holding onto hate and bitterness towards someone will only destroy us in the end. Get rid of it!

Forgiving and Having Mercy For Ourselves
Sometimes I think our worst enemy is ourselves, but its mostly because the real enemy, Satan, is masterminding the whole scheme. You see, he uses your guilt and possibly pride against you. Here's the deal! You're not perfect either! You will make mistakes, too. Actually, it's OK to not be perfect. As long as you are seeking righteousness and following Jesus, He will work with you. He will help you and develop the person He wants you to be. You're a 'work in progress', so keep moving on!

The worst thing you can do is dwell on your imperfections and continue beating yourself up. You belong to God and you are His vessel. Try something new...forgive and have mercy on yourself! You are a child of the King!

God's Forgiveness and Mercy On Us
I guess what it boils down to is this. As Christians, we are to be 'Christ-like'. When we sin, and we all do, we know to pray to God and ask for His mercy and forgiveness. We are confident to know that... HE DID! At that moment you asked... HE DID! So, if we are to be like Him, we need to do the same... to EVERYONE!

Prevent Satan from having a foothold in our lives. Let's share the things God gives us every day... FORGIVENESS and MERCY. Start by pouring yourself some... and then share!

Ahh... refreshing!